AF605648

MICHELLE FAGONE

AIR FRYER ESSENTIALS

FAMILY FAVOURITES

To my two weird and fantastic girls, who are growing up way too fast:
I wish you a life of good food and great love.

To my crazy and supportive husband: Thanks for making me laugh for over twenty years.
Your dry, witty humor is the perfect yin to my slapstick and low-brow yang.

To my insane parents: Thanks for always loving me, taking my side, and keeping me right-ish.

AIR FRYER ESSENTIALS: FAMILY FAVOURITES
First published in Australia in 2022 by
Simon & Schuster (Australia) Pty Limited
Suite 19A, Level 1, Building C, 450 Miller Street, Cammeray, NSW 2062
First published in the United States in 2018 as *The Everything Air Fryer Cookbook* by Adams Media,
an imprint of Simon & Schuster, Inc.

10 9 8 7 6 5 4 3 2 1

Sydney New York London Toronto New Delhi
Visit our website at www.simonandschuster.com.au

Always follow safety and commonsense cooking protocols while using kitchen utensils, operating ovens and stoves, and handling uncooked food. If children are assisting in the preparation of any recipe, they should always be supervised by an adult.

A catalogue record for this book is available from the National Library of Australia

ISBN: 9781761105722

Author: Michelle Fagone of CavegirlCuisine.com
Cover design: Meng Koach
Cover image: Lawrence Furzey
Internal design: Colleen Cunningham
Internal photographs: James Stefiuk
Printed and bound in China by Leo Paper Products

Contents

Introduction

We all know that deep-fried foods are bad for us on so many levels, but there is something about that crunch that is so satisfying. The food is tasty, the meals are convenient, but eating this way is not a lifestyle that our bodies can maintain.

Make the decision to choose fresher foods and to cook them in a healthier manner — with an air fryer! It's true that the air fryer won't produce the exact same thing as breaded, deep-fried food, but it comes close. And instead of grease, you'll be tasting the actual ingredients while still achieving that satisfying crunch.

This cookbook will not only provide you with over 100 easy-to-follow, simple-to-prepare recipes, but it will also give you the tools you need to start preparing air-fried foods. And don't think that all foods are battered and "fried" in this cookbook. You will learn to air-bake muffins and cakes, air-roast chicken and vegetables, and even air-grill beef and seafood.

By cooking in an air fryer, you will be using a significantly lower amount of oil in the preparation of your food, but the heat will still give your food that crispiness on all sides. In addition, because air fryers have a quicker cooking time, more nutrients will stay intact.

Since you can taste more of your actual food, you can start experimenting with herbs and seasonings to impart great flavour instead of relying solely on grease. And while some recipes in this book call for bottled ingredients, most recipes have sidebars on how to make those ingredients from scratch, eliminating fillers and preservatives that are often needed to give those products a stable shelf life. And don't forget to flip through Chapter 5 to find many quick and delicious homemade dips and sauces.

So, are you ready to dive in and learn to cook with this convenient appliance? Read on and start cooking delicious, healthier meals.

Air Fryer Essentials

The air fryer is an easy, healthier alternative to conventional fryers and will quickly become your go-to appliance in your kitchen. The air fryer is so much more versatile than you might think — it's not just useful for those French fries and onion rings! In fact, there's an air-fried meal for almost every taste, diet or mood from breakfast to desserts and everything in between. But before you get to cooking, you'll need to know about your new appliance. This chapter will cover not only what an air fryer is and the benefits of using one, but also what to look for when purchasing an air fryer and tips on how to use and clean it.

What Is an Air Fryer?

Air fryers work by baking foods with a constant stream of hot air circulating around the food, cooking it evenly and quickly, crisping up edges as it does its job. An air fryer cooks foods quicker than a conventional oven, doesn't heat up your living space and is easy to clean. Although similar to a convection oven, an air fryer is smaller in size and convenient to place on the benchtop. And while both these appliances use hot air and cook food from all angles, the air fryer utilises Rapid Air Technology, circulating the heat with speed.

Using an air fryer is not only a better alternative for your health but for your safety as well. Unlike a traditional deep fryer, which can be a fire hazard and should be used with extreme caution, most air fryers have an automatic shut-off feature. Air fryers also offer quick and safe cooking so you don't anguish over oil spills or cooking on an open flame.

The Benefits of Air Frying

There are many reasons to give up traditionally cooked fried foods, which are prepared by submerging foods in heated oil. Fried foods are high in bad fats and kilojoules. Also, when oil is heated beyond its smoke point — the temperature at which an oil begins to smoke, as with deep-frying — certain oils break down and produce toxic fumes and free radicals. In addition, deep-frying foods is just messy, with its splatter in your kitchen or even on you!

In addition to the health benefits of air frying, you'll find there are a few other benefits as well:

It won't heat up your whole house/apartment. When cooking casseroles or thicker cuts of meat, your traditional oven can warm up, providing a heat source that is not always welcome, especially on those long, hot summer days.

It's faster than your oven. Although it's not as fast as a deep fat fryer, the air fryer has quicker cooking times than an oven due to the circulating heat. This is particularly nice for your busy family when your tribe is hungry. Instead of trying to calm your "hangry" (hungry + angry) crowd, reduce your cook time and get those bellies filled with quick and tasty recipes.

It can help with picky eaters. Picky vegetable eaters or parents of picky vegetable eaters can find benefit in the transformative ways of the air fryer. A little breading and a fresh dip can turn zucchini into tasty fries. And a little cornflake breading can be the gateway recipe from fish fingers to a simple salmon fillet. So be creative and get everyone involved.

It's portable. A benefit of cooking in the air fryer is that it is contained. So for those hit-the-road, no-boundaries renegades, the air fryer is perfect in your campervan. No need to worry about splashing hot soup or sizzling bacon burning your skin.

It also works wonders on frozen foods. While the microwave is faster, it doesn't create that crunchy exterior. The air fryer is great on frozen foods such as French fries, fish fingers or spring rolls. As a general rule, cut the cooking time in half of what is recommended on the package. If more cooking time is needed, slowly increase the time by a minute or two so as to not overcook the final product.

When Purchasing an Air Fryer

Fortunately and unfortunately there are several brands, sizes and shapes of air fryers. This book was based on a four-person air fryer, which is the typical middle-of-the-road size. There are larger models and there are smaller ones as well. Depending on your chosen model, the size of your food batches will vary, but cooking times should not be affected. Conveniently, until you find your groove with your appliance, you can just pull out your basket during the cooking process and check the results to view if the food needs extra cooking.

There are a variety of settings offered by the different models. Some of the newest types offer digital settings that allow the user to be in control of the temperature and time. Other models have analogue dials as well as preset temperatures for a variety of fresh and frozen foods.

As the air fryer basket is going to be used with most of your air-fried foods, finding a model with a basket that has a quick-release button is crucial and will make your life easier. This button helps release the mesh basket containing food from the bottom basket for easy shaking or flipping of the food, which is necessary when using this appliance.

Air Fryer Accessories

Most air fryers come with the basic fryer basket; however, there are many other recipes that can be made with the purchase of a few accessories, including a cake barrel, pizza pan and even a skewer rack. But before you purchase any of these, check two things. One, make sure they work with your size and brand of air fryer. Two, check your cupboards, as you may already have some small, oven-safe dishes that will work in your new appliance.

Here are some of the common air fryer accessories:

- **The Cake Barrel:** The cake barrel accessory comes in both a round and a square version. This non-stick cake pan is used for desserts, casseroles and egg dishes. And as a bonus, both barrels have a handle, making retrieval from the appliance a cinch.

- **The Grill Pan:** The grill pan is a non-stick accessory that replaces the basket on the air fryer and is used for grilling fish, meat and vegetables. The basket is removable from the handle, and the grill pan slides right in its place. Because there are no side walls, the pan allows for a bit more room. Also, with the perforated base, the airflow is able to cook underneath while still providing those beautiful grill lines.

- **The Rack:** This metal holder is a round metal rack that allows for a second layer of food in the air fryer. One non-conventional use is for cooking lightweight food like bacon, which tends to fly around with the airflow. You can turn your rack upside down on top of your bacon to hold it in place while cooking.

- **The Pizza Pan:** The pizza pan is a non-stick shallow pan that allows you to make mini pizzas as well as provides a flat surface for a variety of other recipes, such as biscuits, breads and Dutch pancakes.

- **The Silicone Liners:** Silicone cupcake liners or baking cups are oven safe and great for mini meatloaves, cupcakes, on-the-go frittatas, little quick breads and muffins. They are reusable and dishwasher safe, making clean-up a snap!

- **The Skewer Rack:** The skewer rack contains four metal skewers, which can be used for meat and vegetable shish kebabs. With the food elevated slightly above the fry basket, the cooking time is shortened by allowing more room for the airflow to do its job. Just as you would do before outdoor grilling, if you only have wooden skewers, be sure to soak them in water for about 30 minutes prior to cooking, to avoid burning.

COOKING TIP!

A meat thermometer is one of those fairly inexpensive kitchen gadgets that are well worth the price. You neither want to overcook nor undercook your meats. With the varying shapes and sizes of air fryers, being able to test the internal temperature of your steak, chicken, fish, pork and other meats will help guarantee that your food will be cooked to perfection.

Accessory Removal

Cooking with a pot in an appliance is a great idea until it's time to remove the inserted cooking dish. Because of the tight space, it is almost impossible to use thick oven mitts to reach down and grip the pot evenly without tipping one side of the cooking vessel and spilling the cooked food. There are a few ways around this:

1. Wooden or silicone-tipped tongs are a good purchase for air frying. Because most air fryer baskets and accessories have a non-stick surface, a good pair of non-metal tongs are recommended for helping to flip those larger food items, such as egg rolls, that don't benefit from just a quick shake of the basket, as is the case with most fries and chips.

2. Heat-resistant mini mitts or pinch mitts are small, food-grade silicone oven mitts and are especially helpful when lifting pots, racks and barrels out of an air fryer after the cooking process. They are more heat resistant and less cumbersome than traditional oven mitts, which can prove to be bulky in the tight fryer basket.

Homemade Sling

Creating an aluminium-foil sling is a quick, inexpensive, homemade fix to the problem of lifting a heated dish out of an air fryer. Take a 25cm × 25cm square of aluminium foil and fold it until you have a 5cm × 25cm sling. Place this sling underneath the bowl or pan before cooking so that you can easily lift up the heated dish.

Oil and Your Air Fryer

One of the main and obvious benefits when first deciding to purchase an air fryer is the fact that you no longer want to consume deep-fried foods, whether for health purposes or weight issues. But oil and butter are still used in some air frying, just not to the extent that deep-frying calls for. Some recipes in this book will advise to "lightly grease" a pan. Because this seems to be such a personal choice in this day and age, use your preferred method and oil type.

And although your grill basket is most likely of the non-stick variety, a light spritz or brush of oil directly on the basket is necessary with some foods, as indicated in the recipes. Try to avoid using commercial non-stick sprays, as they may contain chemicals that can cause your basket to get sticky or start to flake. True oils and butter, without additives, yield better results.

To avoid heavy drizzling of oil on your food, purchase one of the many types of misters, sprayers and spritzers in which you can use your oil of choice to lightly spray onto foods to encourage browning and crisping. Many prefer this to commercial spray oil, which may contain chemicals and preservatives that may have a denigrating effect on the non-stick components and accessories of your air fryer.

A basting or silicone pastry brush uses more oil than a sprayer does but is helpful on certain dishes that require a brush of melted butter on the dough or breaded food, such as filo tarts or biscuits.

If you want to cut back on the oil even more, instead of giving your basket a light spray or brush of oil, simply cut a piece of parchment paper to the size of the bottom of your basket. It will help keep the batter or other ingredient on your items without adding additional kilojoules.

Air Frying Tips

Although the air fryer is an easy appliance to use, there is always a learning curve associated with any new cooking method. The first rule is that you shouldn't overcrowd your fryer basket. Most foods will have to be cooked in batches to yield the best crunch. You will also have to take this into consideration when purchasing your air fryer. How big is your family? How large are the batches that you'll be preparing? The larger the air fryer capacity, the larger the batches and the quicker the results.

Once the batches are in the air fryer, it is essential to flip or shake the food at least once or more during the cooking process.

This will ensure that the circulating air will touch all sides of the food. After the first flip, some foods, especially those that need to be browned, may need a brush or spritz of oil or butter. That's right: although you are giving up the deep-frying oil, a fraction is required for maximum crispiness.

Smoke and Your Air Fryer

Some fattier cuts of meat, like bacon or marbled steaks, will render fat when cooking. This can create white smoke and can be eliminated by adding 1 to 2 tablespoons of water in the fryer drawer prior to cooking. If it happens in the middle of your cooking time and you didn't anticipate smoke, simply open the drawer and add needed water. If there is black smoke present, unplug the machine and determine the culprit, as food could have attached itself to the heating element, causing the smoke. Remove the rogue food immediately, clean and continue cooking.

Sweat the Small Stuff!

Air frying isn't just about the frying, or even the baking, roasting and grilling. It's about the small stuff, too. Before garnishing an Asian stir-fry with cashews, give them a quick toss in sesame oil and air-fry them for a surprising flavourful crunch. Before enjoying a fresh tomato soup, make some quick grilled cheese croutons to create big smiles. Toast pine nuts for another dimension of flavour before pulsing them into a fresh pesto. The air fryer is one of those appliances that will not only feel right at home on your benchtop but will not collect dust waiting to be used.

Cleaning and Seasoning Your Air Fryer

After using your air fryer, unplug the appliance and allow it to completely cool. Adding cooler water to a hot fryer basket can cause warping. Although the removable parts are dishwasher safe, some people suggest washing the parts by hand with warm, soapy water to lengthen the life of those non-stick, coated parts. Wipe down and remove excess fat or oil from the warming drawer and non-removable parts, inside and out, with hot water and a dishcloth or kitchen sponge.

Also, once dry, the basket can be seasoned. Oftentimes you only hear about this term with cast-iron pans, but the air fryer basket can also benefit from seasoning. Place your air fryer basket in the appliance and heat for 5 minutes at 200°C. Remove the basket and, when cool enough to touch, simply spread a thin layer of coconut oil on your basket using a paper towel. Heat the basket in the appliance for an additional 2 minutes. This will help extend the life of the non-stick coating on the basket.

2

Breakfast

Pork Sausage Patties

It's not only easy to make your own sausage, but you can also control what goes into the food. This sausage can be made in larger batches and can be easily frozen for future morning meals!

- **Hands-On Time:** 10 minutes
- **Cook Time:** 20 minutes

Makes 8 cups

340 grams lean pork mince
1 teaspoon fresh thyme leaves
3/4 tablespoon brown sugar
Pinch ground nutmeg
1/4 teaspoon salt
1/4 teaspoon freshly ground black pepper
3/4 tablespoon water

1. Preheat air fryer at 180°C for 3 minutes.
2. In a large bowl, combine pork, thyme, sugar, nutmeg, salt and pepper. Form into eight patties.
3. Pour water into bottom of air fryer. Place four patties in fryer basket and cook for 5 minutes. Flip patties. Cook for an additional 5 minutes. Repeat with remaining patties.
4. Transfer to a plate and serve warm.

PER SERVING

KILOJOULES: 242 | **FAT:** 1.6g | **PROTEIN:** 8.9g | **SODIUM:** 97mg
FIBRE: 0.0g | **CARBOHYDRATES:** 1.2 G | **SUGAR:** 1.1g

Spicy Scotch Eggs

A Scotch egg is a gastropub classic made by forming sausage or meat around a cooked egg, coating it in bread crumbs and then deep-frying it. With the air fryer, you skip the bath in hot oil and go straight for the goodness without all of the guilt.

- **Hands-On Time:** 5 minutes
- **Cook Time:** 12 minutes

Makes 4 eggs

230 grams chorizo mince, loose or removed from casings
4 soft-boiled eggs, peeled
1 large egg
1 cup plain bread crumbs

1. Preheat air fryer at 190°C for 3 minutes.
2. Gently form chorizo around peeled eggs.
3. In a small bowl, whisk large egg. In another small bowl, add bread crumbs.
4. Dip chorizo-covered eggs in whisked egg and then coat in bread crumbs.
5. Place eggs in air fryer basket. Cook for 6 minutes. Turn. Cook for an additional 6 minutes. Serve warm.

PER SERVING

KILOJOULES: 1347 | **FAT:** 22.2 g | **PROTEIN:** 19.7 g |
SODIUM: 775mg | **FIBRE:** 0.3g | **CARBOHYDRATES:** 6.2g |
SUGAR: 0.7g

Air-Fried Maple Bacon

What's better than bacon? Maple bacon! This sweet and salty treat will wake you up with a smile. It's also delicious on breakfast sandwiches, crumbled up into your favourite salads and even dipped in a little chocolate for some bacon candy. Sinful, truly sinful!

- **Hands-On Time:** 5 minutes
- **Cook Time:** 12 minutes

Serves 4

2 tablespoons water
4 slices bacon, halved
2 teaspoons maple syrup, divided

1 Preheat air fryer at 200°C for 3 minutes.

2 Pour water into bottom of air fryer. Place 4 bacon halves in air fryer basket. Cook for 3 minutes. Flip bacon. Brush 1 teaspoon maple syrup on bacon. Cook for an additional 3 minutes. Transfer to a paper towel-lined plate.

3 Repeat with remaining bacon and serve warm.

PER SERVING

KILOJOULES: 213 | **FAT:** 3.0g | **PROTEIN:** 3.6g | **SODIUM:** 162mg | **FIBRE:** 0.0g | **CARBOHYDRATES:** 2.2g | **SUGAR:** 2.0g

Soft-"Boiled" Eggs

For a full, healthy breakfast experience, serve the soft-"boiled" eggs with a plate of fresh fruit and steamed asparagus. Steamed asparagus? Oh, yes, the spears are divine dipped in the gooey deliciousness of that heavenly yolk.

- **Hands-On Time:** 5 minutes
- **Cook Time:** 8 minutes

Makes 4 soft-"boiled" eggs

4 large eggs
1 cup ice
1 cup water

HARD-"BOILED" EGGS!

If you don't like a soft runny centre, simply leave the eggs in the air fryer for 15 minutes.

1 Preheat air fryer at 120°C for 3 minutes.

2 Place eggs in silicone muffin cups to avoid eggs from bumping around and cracking during the cooking process. Add eggs in cups to air fryer basket. Cook for 8 minutes.

3 Add ice and water to a medium bowl. Transfer eggs to this water bath immediately to stop the cooking process. After 5 minutes, peel and eat.

PER SERVING

KILOJOULES: 297 | **FAT:** 4.3g | **PROTEIN:** 6.3g | **SODIUM:** 148mg | **FIBRE:** 0.0g | **CARBOHYDRATES:** 0.4g | **SUGAR:** 0.2g

Individual Egg and Cheese Soufflés

Serve these immediately so you can enjoy the "fluff". Also, don't be afraid to change up the ingredients in the bottom of your ramekin. Try chopped mushrooms, cooked sausage, diced avocado or whatever else your taste buds request!

- **Hands-On Time:** 5 minutes
- **Cook Time:** 10 minutes

Serves 3

¼ cup chopped deli ham
¼ cup diced tomato
1 ½ tablespoons chopped spring onions
3 large eggs
1 ½ tablespoons full-cream milk
¼ teaspoon salt
¼ teaspoon freshly ground black pepper
⅛ teaspoon smoked paprika

1. Preheat air fryer at 140°C for 3 minutes.
2. Lightly grease three 200ml ramekins. Divide cheese, ham, tomato and spring onions equally among the ramekins.
3. In a small bowl, whisk eggs, milk, salt, pepper and paprika. Pour into ramekins.
4. Add ramekins to air fryer basket. Cook for 10 minutes.
5. Serve immediately while still fluffy.

PER SERVING

KILOJOULES: 502 | **FAT:** 7.9g | **PROTEIN:** 9.9g | **SODIUM:** 485mg | **FIBRE:** 0.5g | **CARBOHYDRATES:** 2.4g | **SUGAR:** 1.4g

Breakfast Tarts

Puff pastry can be found in the freezer section of your supermarket. Thaw it out, slice it, add your favourite toppings, air-fry and then enjoy this meal for a scrumptious "brinner" (brunch plus dinner) served with a light salad or some fresh fruit!

- **Hands-On Time:** 15 minutes
- **Cook Time:** 26 minutes

Makes 6 tarts

110 grams lean pork mince
¼ teaspoon rubbed sage
¼ teaspoon brown sugar
Pinch cayenne pepper
Pinch ground nutmeg
¼ teaspoon salt
¾ tablespoon plain flour
1 sheet puff pastry, thawed to room temperature
1 large egg, whisked
4 large eggs, scrambled
½ cup shredded Cheddar cheese

1. In a large frying pan over medium-high heat, cook pork for 2 minutes, chopping it as the pork cooks. Add sage, sugar, cayenne pepper, nutmeg and salt. Continue to stir-fry for 2–3 minutes until pork is no longer pink.
2. Scatter flour over a flat, clean surface. Unfold puff pastry sheet on the floured surface. Cut into six equal rectangles. Brush each rectangle perimeter with whisked egg.
3. Top each rectangle with even amounts pork mixture, scrambled eggs and shredded cheese.
4. Preheat air fryer at 180°C for 3 minutes.
5. Place two tarts at a time in lightly greased air fryer basket. Cook for 7 minutes. Repeat with remaining tarts. Serve warm.

PER SERVING

KILOJOULES: 861 | **FAT:** 11.9 g | **PROTEIN:** 15.9 g | **SODIUM:** 269 mg | **FIBRE:** 0.2 g | **CARBOHYDRATES:** 5.5 g | **SUGAR:** 0.8 g

Baked Oatmeal

This breakfast treat is not only full of flavour, its oats have a low glycemic index and are slow to digest, improving your satiety. Slice and serve as is or scoop out a portion to a bowl and pour your preferred milk around the baked oatmeal.

- **Hands-On Time:** 10 minutes
- **Cook Time:** 8 minutes

Serves 4

1 1/2 cups quick-cooking oats
1/3 cup packed light brown sugar
1 large egg
1 teaspoon fresh orange zest
3/4 tablespoon freshly squeezed orange juice
1 1/2 tablespoons full-cream milk
1 1/2 tablespoons pure maple syrup
1 1/2 tablespoons unsalted butter, melted
1/4 cup raisins
Pinch ground nutmeg
Pinch salt
1/4 cup pecan pieces

1. Preheat air fryer at 160°C for 3 minutes.
2. In a medium bowl, combine all the ingredients. Transfer mixture to a greased cake barrel (accessory).
3. Place pan in fryer basket and cook for 8 minutes.
4. Transfer to a cooling rack for 5 minutes. Slice and serve warm.

PER SERVING

KILOJOULES: 1518 | **FAT:** 13.0g | **PROTEIN:** 6.9g | **SODIUM:** 66mg
FIBRE: 4.2g | **CARBOHYDRATES:** 55.4g | **SUGAR:** 31.3g

Dutch Baby Pancake with Fresh Blackberries

Sometimes called a German pancake or a Dutch puff, this hybrid of a pancake and a popover is a tasty breakfast and can be served with toppings only limited by your imagination. Serve a chilled mimosa with this treat for a special brunch on a slow morning.

- **Hands-On Time:** 10 minutes
- **Cook Time:** 10 minutes

Makes 1 large pancake

¼ cup plain flour
¼ cup full-cream milk
1 large egg
1 tablespoon sugar
½ teaspoon vanilla extract
¼ teaspoon salt
¼ teaspoon ground cinnamon
¾ tablespoon unsalted butter
¾ tablespoon icing sugar
¼ cup fresh blackberries
¾ tablespoon pure maple syrup

BLACKBERRIES FOR HEALTH

The magnesium in blackberries can do amazing things for respiratory relief but can also help create stronger bones. This powerful mineral plays an important role in the absorption of calcium, and a diet rich in magnesium ensures strong bones.

1. In a medium bowl, combine flour, milk, egg, sugar, vanilla, salt and cinnamon.
2. Preheat air fryer at 200°C for 3 minutes with pizza pan (accessory) in the air fryer. After preheating, add butter and push it to coat pan as it melts.
3. Add batter to pan. Cook for 10 minutes. The pancake will be puffed up when done but will fall immediately after it comes out of the air fryer.
4. Transfer pancake to a plate. Sprinkle with icing sugar. Add blackberries and drizzle with maple syrup. Serve warm.

PER SERVING

KILOJOULES: 1924 | **FAT:** 17.0g | **PROTEIN:** 11.6g | **SODIUM:** 681mg | **FIBRE:** 1.2g | **CARBOHYDRATES:** 61.8g **SUGAR:** 36.0 g

Crab and Goat Cheese Frittata

This crustless creation is naturally gluten-free and will have your taste buds dancing for joy. This frittata is a flavour powerhouse with the sweetness from the beautiful lump crab, the creaminess of the goat cheese, the intense pungent bite of the horseradish, and the freshness of the mint and lemon juice.

- **Hands-On Time:** 10 minutes
- **Cook Time:** 14 minutes

Serves 2

5 large eggs
¼ teaspoon salt
¼ teaspoon freshly ground black pepper
1 teaspoon prepared horseradish
¼ cup brown onion, finely chopped
¼ cup lump crabmeat, picked over and any shells discarded
⅓ cup crumbled goat cheese
1 ½ tablespoons chopped fresh mint
¼ teaspoon lemon juice

1. Preheat air fryer at 160°C for 3 minutes.
2. In a medium bowl, whisk eggs. Stir in remaining ingredients. Pour into lightly greased cake barrel (accessory).
3. Cook for 14 minutes. Transfer to a cooling rack for 5 minutes. Slice and serve warm.

PER SERVING

KILOJOULES: 1384 | **FAT:** 21.0 g | **PROTEIN:** 26.7 g | **SODIUM:** 721 mg | **FIBRE:** 0.6 g | **CARBOHYDRATES:** 3.6 g | **SUGAR:** 1.6 g

Cubano Strata

After cooking a pork shoulder or butt for those barbecue sandwiches, set aside some of the meat before adding the sauce. You'll have enough for this breakfast tribute to the tasty and amazing Cuban sandwich.

- **Hands-On Time:** 10 minutes
- **Cook Time:** 14 minutes

Serves 2

5 large eggs
1/4 teaspoon salt
1/4 teaspoon freshly ground black pepper
1 teaspoon yellow mustard
3/4 tablespoon dill pickle relish
1/4 cup finely diced cooked ham
1/4 cup shredded cooked pork
1/3 cup grated Swiss cheese
2 slices sandwich bread, diced

1. Preheat air fryer at 160°C for 3 minutes.
2. In a medium bowl, whisk eggs. Stir in remaining ingredients. Pour into lightly greased cake barrel (accessory).
3. Cook for 14 minutes. Transfer to a cooling rack for 5 minutes. Slice and serve warm.

PER SERVING

KILOJOULES: 1740 | **FAT:** 21.5g | **PROTEIN:** 31.2g | **SODIUM:** 990 mg | **FIBRE:** 1.1 g | **CARBOHYDRATES:** 18.9 g | **SUGAR:** 2.4 g

Bacony Brunch Frittata

There's nothing more indulgent than wearing your pyjamas all day, eating off a tray in bed and binge-watching that series you've been meaning to get to. Well, make a date with yourself, sleep in late and enjoy this tasty frittata.

- **Hands-On Time:** 10 minutes
- **Cook Time:** 14 minutes

Serves 2

5 large eggs
¼ teaspoon salt
¼ teaspoon freshly ground black pepper
½ cup baby spinach
¼ cup brown onion, finely chopped
4 slices cooked bacon, crumbled
1 medium Roma tomato, diced
¼ cup grated mozzarella cheese

1. Preheat air fryer at 160°C for 3 minutes.
2. In a medium bowl, whisk eggs. Stir in remaining ingredients. Pour into lightly greased cake barrel (accessory).
3. Cook for 14 minutes. Transfer to a cooling rack for 5 minutes. Slice and serve warm.

PER SERVING

KILOJOULES: 1422 | **FAT:** 21.5g | **PROTEIN:** 27.3g | **SODIUM:** 950mg
FIBRE: 1.0g | **CARBOHYDRATES:** 5.1g | **SUGAR:** 2.3g

Loaded Avocado Toast

There is a reason that everyone's been talking about avocado toast. It is delicious! Now load it up with other goodies, like fresh tomatoes and creamy goat cheese, and you won't want to eat anything else for breakfast ... ever!

- **Hands-On Time:** 10 minutes
- **Cook Time:** 10 minutes

Serves 2

1 medium avocado, peeled and pitted
1 clove garlic, minced
¼ teaspoon lime juice
Pinch salt
2 slices wholegrain bread
2 medium Campari tomatoes, sliced
¼ teaspoon freshly ground black pepper
3 tablespoons goat cheese, crumbled

1. In a small bowl, using the back of a fork, press and combine avocado, garlic, lime juice and salt until smooth.
2. Preheat air fryer at 180°C for 3 minutes.
3. Spread avocado mixture over bread. Add tomato slices. Sprinkle with pepper and top with goat cheese.
4. Place 1 piece topped bread in air fryer basket. Cook for 5 minutes. Transfer to a plate. Repeat with remaining bread and serve warm.

PER SERVING

KILOJOULES: 1129 | **FAT:** 14.4g | **PROTEIN:** 9.6g | **SODIUM:** 287 mg | **FIBRE:** 8.1 g | **CARBOHYDRATES:** 25.1 g | **SUGAR:** 4.9 g

Breads and Baked Goods

Chocolate-Espresso Muffins

When you need your chocolate and coffee all in one, and you need it to go, grab one of these muffins and hit the road. Sweet, rich and quick are just what some mornings call for!

- **Hands-On Time:** 10 minutes
- **Cook Time:** 7 minutes

Serves 6

½ cup plain flour
¼ cup unsweetened cocoa powder
2 teaspoons instant espresso powder
1 teaspoon baking powder
½ teaspoon bi-carb soda
¼ cup sugar
Pinch salt
½ teaspoon vanilla extract
2 ¼ tablespoons unsalted butter, melted
2 large eggs
1 ½ tablespoons full-cream milk

1. In a large bowl, combine flour, cocoa powder, espresso powder, baking powder, bi-carb soda, sugar and salt.
2. In a medium bowl, combine vanilla, butter, eggs and milk.
3. Preheat air fryer at 190°C for 3 minutes.
4. Pour wet ingredients from the medium bowl into the large bowl of dry ingredients. Gently combine ingredients. Do not overmix. Spoon mixture into six lightly greased silicone cupcake liners.
5. Cook for 7 minutes. Transfer silicone muffins to a cooling rack. Serve warm or cooled.

PER SERVING

KILOJOULES: 661 | **FAT:** 7.5g | **PROTEIN:** 4.1 | **SODIUM:** 237mg
FIBRE: 1.6g | **CARBOHYDRATES:** 19.2g | **SUGAR:** 8.8g

Chocolate-Strawberry Muffins

Inspired by chocolate-covered strawberries, these muffins are just the ticket when you're craving a doughnut but want to skip the over-the-top kilojoule count. For a variation, use dark, unsweetened cocoa. It will yield a rich blackish colour and there is definitely a flavour difference.

- **Hands-On Time:** 10 minutes
- **Cook Time:** 7 minutes

Serves 4

1/2 cup plain flour
1/4 cup unsweetened cocoa powder
1/2 teaspoon bi-carb soda
1/4 cup sugar
Pinch salt
1/2 teaspoon vanilla extract
2 1/4 tablespoons butter, melted
2 large eggs
1 1/2 tablespoons full-cream milk
1/4 cup minced strawberries

1. In a large bowl, combine flour, cocoa powder, bi-carb soda, sugar and salt.
2. In a medium bowl, combine vanilla, butter, eggs, milk and strawberries.
3. Preheat air fryer at 190°C for 3 minutes.
4. Pour wet ingredients from the medium bowl into the large bowl of dry ingredients. Gently combine ingredients. Do not overmix. Spoon mixture into six lightly greased silicone cupcake liners.
5. Cook for 7 minutes. Transfer silicone muffins to a cooling rack. Serve warm or cooled.

PER SERVING

KILOJOULES: 661 | **FAT:** 7.5g | **PROTEIN:** 4.1g | **SODIUM:** 156mg
FIBRE: 1.7g | **CARBOHYDRATES:** 19.3g | **SUGAR:** 9.1g

Artisanal Olive Bread

For lovers of the humble and briny olive, this is your bread. This Mediterranean-style crusty loaf is perfect with steamed mussels, a bowl of pasta or even sliced for a fresh mozzarella and tomato sandwich (crisped and melted to perfection in your air fryer)!

- **Hands-On Time:** 10 minutes
- **Cook Time:** 40 minutes

Serves 6

1 teaspoon active dry yeast
1 cup warm water
2 ½ cups plain flour
1 ½ teaspoons salt
¼ cup finely diced pitted Kalamata olives
¾ tablespoon chopped fresh dill
1 ½ tablespoons water
1 teaspoon olive oil

1. In a large bowl add yeast and warm water. Stir until yeast is dissolved. Add flour, salt, olives and dill. Stir until a dough forms. It will look messy and loose, not a perfect ball, and this is good. Seal top of bowl with plastic wrap and let sit on the kitchen counter for 10 hours.
2. Preheat air fryer at 200°C for 10 minutes with round cake barrel (accessory) in the air fryer as well. Place 1½ tablespoons water in bottom drip pan after preheating the device.
3. Flour your hands and carefully form the dough into a ball but don't overmix it. Place ball into heated cake barrel. Lightly press down on top of ball to slightly flatten. Cover dish with aluminium foil. Cook for 30 minutes.
4. Remove foil and lightly brush top of bread with olive oil. Cook for an additional 10 minutes. Transfer to a cooling rack.
5. Serve warm or at room temperature.

PER SERVING

KILOJOULES: 907 | **FAT:** 3.0g | **PROTEIN:** 5.8g | **SODIUM:** 685mg | **FIBRE:** 1.8g | **CARBOHYDRATES:** 40.6g | **SUGAR:** 0.1g

No-Knead Crusty Bread

Crispy on the outside and soft on the inside, this crusty bread will rival any artisanal bread you can buy at the bakery. Just combine ingredients and allow to rise overnight. There is no kneading required in the making of this simple bread and the results are very tasty!

- **Hands-On Time:** 10 minutes
- **Cook Time:** 40 minutes

Serves 6

1 teaspoon active dry yeast
1 cup warm water
2 ½ cups plain flour
1 ½ teaspoons salt
1 ½ tablespoons water
1 teaspoon olive oil

1. In a large bowl add yeast and warm water. Stir until yeast is dissolved. Add flour and salt and stir until a dough forms. It will look messy and loose, not a perfect ball, and this is good. Seal top of bowl with plastic wrap and let sit on the kitchen counter for 10 hours.
2. Preheat air fryer at 200°C for 10 minutes with round cake barrel (accessory) in the air fryer as well. Place 1½ tablespoons water in bottom drip pan after preheating the device.
3. Flour your hands and carefully form the dough into a ball but don't overmix it. Place ball into heated cake barrel. Lightly press down on top of ball to slightly flatten. Cover dish with aluminium foil. Cook for 30 minutes.
4. Remove foil and lightly brush top of bread with olive oil. Cook for an additional 10 minutes. Transfer to a cooling rack.
5. Serve warm or at room temperature.

PER SERVING

KILOJOULES: 828 | **FAT:** 1.1g | **PROTEIN:** 5.7g | **SODIUM:** 582mg | **FIBRE:** 1.6g | **CARBOHYDRATES:** 40.0g | **SUGAR:** 0.1g

Cheddar Dinner Rolls

Let's face it, Cheddar cheese goes with almost any dish, but you can get creative with other cheese varieties as well in these rolls. Swiss cheese would complement a ham meal. Fetta cheese would be nice with a Greek salad. And try blue cheese with a steak dish for a sharp contrast.

- **Hands-On Time:** 15 minutes
- **Cook Time:** 18 minutes

Makes 8 rolls

1 teaspoon active dry yeast
¼ cup warm water
2 cups plain flour
1 teaspoon salt
¾ tablespoon Italian seasoning
2 teaspoons sugar
1 large egg
⅓ cup full-cream milk
¼ cup shredded Cheddar cheese
2 ¼ tablespoons butter, melted and divided
1 teaspoon olive oil

1. In a large bowl add yeast and water. Stir until yeast is dissolved. Stir in flour, salt, seasoning and sugar. Add egg, milk, cheese and 1 tablespoon melted butter. Use a fork to combine until a dough starts to form. Transfer dough to a floured flat, clean surface. Knead dough 5 minutes. Form into a ball.
2. Brush olive oil on a medium bowl. Add dough. Cover with a damp cloth and set aside 1 hour.
3. Punch down dough and transfer to a floured flat, clean surface.
4. Preheat air fryer at 190°C for 3 minutes.
5. Separate dough into eight sections. Roll each section into a ball. Place four balls in lightly greased pizza pan (accessory). Cook for 7 minutes. Brush 1 tablespoon melted butter on tops of rolls. Cook for an additional 2 minutes. Repeat with remaining rolls and butter.
6. Transfer to a cooling rack. Serve warm.

PER SERVING

KILOJOULES: 778 | **FAT:** 6.1g | **PROTEIN:** 5.4g | **SODIUM:** 327mg | **FIBRE:** 1.0g | **CARBOHYDRATES:** 25.7g | **SUGAR:** 1.7g

Soft Pretzel Breadsticks

Make these easy pretzel breadsticks for your next craft beer tasting party! They are equally great served with your next sausage and cabbage meal.

- **Hands-On Time:** 10 minutes
- **Cook Time:** 13 hours

Makes 10 breadsticks

½ cup warm water
2 teaspoons white sugar
1 ½ teaspoons packed brown sugar
1 teaspoon active dry yeast
1 ½ tablespoons vegetable oil
2 cups plain flour
¾ tablespoon olive oil
6 cups water
1 cup bi-carb soda
1 teaspoon salt
1 large egg, whisked
2 teaspoons coarse salt

1. In a large bowl, add warm water, white sugar and brown sugar. Stir until sugars are dissolved. Add yeast. Let stand for 5 minutes. Incorporate vegetable oil and flour into the liquid.
2. Flip sticky dough onto a floured flat, clean work surface. Knead dough for 3 minutes. Brush with olive oil on large bowl and add dough. Cover bowl with a damp cloth and leave alone for 1 hour.
3. Punch down dough. Divide into 10 sections. Roll each section into a breadstick 15cm long.
4. In a large pot, bring 6 cups water, bi-carb soda and salt to a boil. Working in batches of five, add pretzel sticks to water and allow to boil for about 30 seconds each batch. Using a slotted spoon, remove pretzels from water and set aside on a plate. Brush sticks with whisked egg.
5. Preheat air fryer at 190°C for 3 minutes.
6. Place five pretzel sticks in lightly greased air fryer basket and cook for 6 minutes. Transfer to a plate and garnish with half of the coarse salt. Repeat. Serve warm.

PER SERVING

KILOJOULES: 539 | **FAT:** 3.2g | **PROTEIN:** 3.4g | **SODIUM:** 1,193mg | **FIBRE:** 0.8g | **CARBOHYDRATES:** 20.1g | **SUGAR:** 1.6g

Buckwheat Quick Bread

If you are serving a meal out of your cast-iron pan, this buckwheat quick bread will fit right in with its rustic and rich flavour. The addition of the honey adds just enough sweetness to counter the flavour of buckwheat, still making this a savoury bread option.

- **Hands-On Time:** 5 minutes
- **Cook Time:** 7 minutes

Serves 6

1 cup buckwheat flour
1 ½ teaspoons baking powder
⅛ teaspoon garlic powder
½ teaspoon salt
2 ¼ tablespoons butter, melted
½ cup full-cream milk
1 tablespoon honey

1 In a medium bowl, combine all the ingredients.

2 Preheat air fryer at 190°C for 3 minutes.

3 Spread mixture in lightly greased pizza pan (accessory). Cook for 7 minutes.

4 Remove from air fryer and let cool for 10 minutes to set. Serve warm.

PER SERVING

KILOJOULES: 589 | **FAT:** 6.5g | **PROTEIN:** 3.3g | **SODIUM:** 327mg
FIBRE: 2.0g | **CARBOHYDRATES:** 18.3g | **SUGAR:** 4.4g

Banana-Nut Bread

Banana bread has the ability to awaken memories of Grandma. You can bring back a little nostalgia and also get rid of that lone ripe banana in 25 minutes from start to finish!

- **Hands-On Time:** 5 minutes
- **Cook Time:** 8 minutes

Serves 6

1 cup plain flour
1 teaspoon baking powder
¼ teaspoon bi-carb soda
⅓ cup sugar
¼ teaspoon ground cinnamon
¼ teaspoon salt
⅓ cup mashed banana (about 1 large banana)
1 large egg
¾ tablespoon full-cream milk
1 teaspoon vanilla extract
¼ cup pecan pieces

1 In a medium bowl, combine all the ingredients.

2 Preheat air fryer at 190°C for 3 minutes.

3 Spread mixture in lightly greased pizza pan (accessory). Cook for 15 minutes.

4 Remove from air fryer and let cool for 10 minutes to set. Serve warm.

PER SERVING

KILOJOULES: 589 | **FAT:** 6.5g | **PROTEIN:** 3.3g | **SODIUM:** 327mg
FIBRE: 2.0g | **CARBOHYDRATES:** 18.3g | **SUGAR:** 4.4g

Zucchini Chocolate Chip Bread

This recipe is essential when your garden is overflowing with zucchini. Because this bread has a similar taste to banana bread, your picky eaters will never know the difference, especially with the addition of chocolate chips. Who can resist that?!

- **Hands-On Time:** 10 minutes
- **Cook Time:** 15 minutes

Serves 6

1 cup plain flour
1 teaspoon baking powder
1/4 teaspoon bi-carb soda
1/2 cup sugar
1/4 teaspoon ground cinnamon
1/4 teaspoon salt
1/3 cup grated zucchini
1 large egg
3/4 tablespoon full-cream milk
1 teaspoon vanilla extract
1/4 cup chocolate chips

1. In a medium bowl, combine all the ingredients.
2. Preheat air fryer at 190°C for 3 minutes.
3. Spread mixture in lightly greased pizza pan (accessory). Cook for 15 minutes.
4. Remove from air fryer and let cool for 10 minutes to set. Serve warm.

PER SERVING

KILOJOULES: 807 | **FAT:** 3.1g | **PROTEIN:** 3.7g | **SODIUM:** 245mg | **FIBRE:** 1.1g | **CARBOHYDRATES:** 38.2g | **SUGAR:** 21.2g

Bacon and Cheese Dumpling Bites

Serve these bites alongside your favourite eggs and a thick slice of tomato and sautéd mushrooms. Your family will scream for these savoury, fluffy dumplings every weekend.

- **Hands-On Time:** 10 minutes
- **Cook Time:** 12 minutes

Makes 9 dumplings

1/3 cup plain flour
1/4 teaspoon salt
1/4 teaspoon baking powder
1/2 cup cooked, crumbled bacon
56 grams cream cheese, at room temperature
1/4 cup shredded sharp Cheddar cheese
1 teaspoon chopped chives
1 1/2 tablespoons buttermilk
1/2 teaspoon vegetable oil

1. In a medium bowl, combine flour, salt and baking powder.
2. In a small bowl, combine remaining ingredients and stir until smooth. Add ingredients from small bowl to dry ingredients in medium bowl. Do not overmix.
3. Preheat air fryer at 160°C for 3 minutes.
4. Form mixture into nine (3cm) balls and add to pizza pan (accessory). It's alright if the biscuits are touching. Cook for 12 minutes.
5. Transfer to a plate. Serve warm.

PER SERVING

KILOJOULES: 426 | **FAT:** 6.5g | **PROTEIN:** 5.2g | **SODIUM:** 296mg
FIBRE: 0.1g | **CARBOHYDRATES:** 4.2g | **SUGAR:** 0.4g

Pull-Apart Buttermilk Scones

When cooking, scones actually fluff up higher when placed beside each other. So crowd that pan. Your taller, fluffy scones will reward you.

- **Hands-On Time:** 10 minutes
- **Cook Time:** 15 minutes

Makes 10 biscuits

2 cups plain flour
2 teaspoons baking powder
1 teaspoon salt
1 ½ tablespoons butter, melted
1 cup buttermilk

1. In a medium bowl, combine flour, baking powder and salt. Add butter and buttermilk until a sticky dough forms.
2. Preheat air fryer at 180°C for 3 minutes.
3. Flour your hands and form mixture evenly into 10 Ping-Pong-sized balls. Add balls to lightly greased pizza pan (accessory) so that they are touching. Cook for 15 minutes.
4. Transfer to a plate. Serve warm.

PER SERVING

KILOJOULES: 523 | **FAT:** 2.8g | **PROTEIN:** 3.6g | **SODIUM:** 356mg
FIBRE: 0.7g | **CARBOHYDRATES:** 20.6g | **SUGAR:** 1.4g

Garlic-Butter Cloverleafs

Cloverleafs are made by placing three balls of dough in one muffin cup. They rise up together during the cooking process, achieving cute little clover-shaped rolls. These cloverleafs are quick to bake and make a great addition to a meat and potatoes meal.

- **Hands-On Time:** 10 minutes
- **Cook Time:** 6 minutes

Makes 4 Cloverleafs

1 cup plain flour

1 1/2 teaspoons baking powder

3/4 teaspoon salt

3 cloves garlic, minced

3 tablespoons full-cream milk

2 1/4 tablespoons butter, melted and divided

1. In a small bowl, combine flour, baking powder and salt. Add garlic, milk and 3/4 tablespoon butter until a sticky dough forms.
2. Preheat air fryer at 180°C for 3 minutes.
3. Lightly grease four silicone muffin cups.
4. Flour your hands and form mixture into 12 balls of equal size. Add three balls to each muffin cup. Place muffin cups in air fryer basket. Cook for 3 minutes. Brush tops of cloverleafs with remaining butter. Cook for an additional 3 minutes.
5. Transfer to a plate. Serve warm.

PER SERVING

KILOJOULES: 849 | **FAT:** 8.7g | **PROTEIN:** 3.9g | **SODIUM:** 626mg
FIBRE: 0.9g | **CARBOHYDRATES:** 25.8g | **SUGAR:** 0.9g

Dilly Dinner Puff Rolls

Light and buttery, the fillo pastry helps accent the very distinct and mildly bitter addition of dill. These puff rolls are amazing paired with salmon, crab cakes, seared scallops or even a crisp summer salad.

- **Hands-On Time:** 15 minutes
- **Cook Time:** 18 minutes

Makes 10 rolls

3/4 tablespoon plain flour

1 sheet fillo pastry, thawed to room temperature

3/4 tablespoon butter, melted

1 1/2 tablespoons grated Parmesan cheese

1 teaspoon garlic salt

2 teaspoons chopped fresh dill

1. Sprinkle flour over a flat, clean surface. Place fillo sheet over scattered flour. Brush butter over sheet.
2. Evenly scatter cheese, garlic salt and dill over fillo sheet. From short end to short end, roll into a log. Refrigerate for 30 minutes. Slice log into 10 equal slices.
3. Preheat air fryer at 180°C for 3 minutes.
4. Place four puff rolls in lightly greased air fryer basket. Cook for 6 minutes. Repeat with remaining puff rolls. Transfer cooked puff rolls to a cooling rack. Serve warm.

PER SERVING

KILOJOULES: 1464 | **FAT:** 1.4g | **PROTEIN:** 0.4g | **SODIUM:** 223mg
FIBRE: 0.0g | **CARBOHYDRATES:** 1.1g | **SUGAR:** 0.0g

Appetisers, Snacks and Sandwiches

Buffalo-Honey Chicken Wings

The sweetness of the honey helps temper the heat from the buffalo sauce, making this a mild combination perfect for the entire family. You may want to make a double batch because these wings disappear in no time.

- **Hands-On Time:** 15 minutes
- **Cook Time:** 44 minutes

Serves 6

1 tablespoon water
910 grams chicken wings, split at the joint, tips removed
3/4 tablespoon butter
1/2 cup buffalo sauce
1 1/2 tablespoons honey

HOW TO SEPARATE CHICKEN WINGS

Some supermarkets sell chicken wings pre-cut; however, you may need to purchase whole chicken wings. To separate, stretch the wing out. There will be three sections, the drumette, the wingette and the tip. Using a sharp knife or kitchen scissors, cut the portions at the joint. The tip is not typically used in chicken wing recipes but you can freeze them and use them at a later date in a broth or to season soups.

1. Place 1 tablespoon water in the bottom of the air fryer to ensure minimum smoke from fat drippings.
2. Preheat air fryer at 120°C for 3 minutes.
3. Place half of wings in air fryer basket. Cook for 6 minutes. Flip wings. Cook for an additional 6 minutes.
4. While wings are cooking, combine butter, wing sauce and honey in a large bowl. The chicken wings will melt the butter, so don't worry about melting it beforehand.
5. Raise temperature on air fryer to 200°C. Flip wings and cook for 5 minutes. Flip wings and cook for an additional 5 minutes. Transfer to bowl with sauce and toss.
6. Repeat process with remaining wings and transfer all to a serving dish.

PER SERVING

KILOJOULES: 1539 | **FAT:** 22.9g | **PROTEIN:** 31.0g | **SODIUM:** 741mg
FIBRE: 0.09g | **CARBOHYDRATES:** 5.8g | **SUGAR:** 5.8g

Thai Sweet Chilli Wings

The crispy skin on these wings from air frying is amazing with the sticky goodness of the sauce. Although you can purchase a similar sauce in the Asian aisle of your supermarket, you'll find a homemade recipe on page 73.

- **Hands-On Time:** 15 minutes
- **Cook Time:** 44 minutes

Serves 6

1 tablespoon water
910 grams chicken wings, split at the joint, tips removed
½ cup Sweet Chilli Sauce (see page 73)

1. Place 1 tablespoon water in the bottom of the air fryer to ensure minimum smoke from fat drippings.
2. Preheat air fryer at 120°C for 3 minutes.
3. Place half of wings in air fryer basket. Cook for 6 minutes. Flip wings. Cook an for additional 6 minutes.
4. While wings are cooking, add sauce to a large bowl.
5. Raise temperature on air fryer to 200°C. Flip wings and cook for 5 minutes. Flip wings and cook for an additional 5 minutes. Transfer to bowl with sauce and toss.
6. Repeat process with remaining wings and transfer all to a serving dish.

PER SERVING

KILOJOULES: 1974 | **FAT:** 21.1g | **PROTEIN:** 31.1g | **SODIUM:** 238mg
FIBRE: 0.0g | **CARBOHYDRATES:** 35.2g | **SUGAR:** 33.6g

Fried Fetta-Dill-Crumbed Kalamata Olives

The familiar combination of fetta, dill and Kalamata olives is concentrated in this one little bite of joy. The crispy exterior dough is perfected in the air fryer. Serve these olives as an appetiser, a snack or even thrown into a fresh Greek salad!

- **Hands-On Time:** 15 minutes
- **Cook Time:** 8 minutes

Serves 5

2/3 cup plain flour
1/2 teaspoon baking powder
1/2 cup fetta cheese, crumbled
1/2 teaspoon dried dill
3 tablespoons butter, melted
25 pitted standard Kalamata olives

1. In a food processor, pulse flour, baking powder, fetta cheese, dill and melted butter until a doughy ball forms.
2. Drain olives and pat dry with a paper towel.
3. Form just enough flour mixture around an olive to cover it. Roll between your hands to form a smooth ball. Repeat with remaining olives.
4. Preheat air fryer at 190°C for 3 minutes.
5. Place olives in lightly greased air fryer basket. Cook for 3 minutes. Gently shake. Cook for an additional 3 minutes. Gently shake. Cook for an additional 2 minutes. Check to see if lightly browned. Give more time if needed; otherwise, transfer to a serving dish and let rest for 5 minutes before serving warm.

PER SERVING

KILOJOULES: 941 | **FAT:** 16.7g | **PROTEIN:** 4.0g | **SODIUM:** 475mg
FIBRE: 0.5g | **CARBOHYDRATES:** 13.5g | **SUGAR:** 0.7g

Pepperoni Pizza Bites

Dip these scrumptious bites in a warm Napoletana sauce as an after-school snack. The salty pepperoni and melty mozzarella create a winning combination.

- **Hands-On Time:** 10 minutes
- **Cook Time:** 12 minutes

Serves 2

1/3 cup plain flour
1/4 teaspoon salt
1/4 teaspoon baking powder
1/2 cup small-diced pepperoni
56 grams cream cheese, at room temperature
1/4 cup shredded mozzarella cheese
1/2 teaspoon Italian seasoning
1 1/2 tablespoons full-cream milk
1 teaspoon olive oil

1. In a small bowl, combine flour, salt and baking powder.
2. In a medium bowl, combine remaining ingredients until smooth. Add dry ingredients until well combined.
3. Preheat air fryer at 160°C for 5 minutes.
4. Form mixture into nine (3cm) balls and add to pizza pan (accessory). It's alright if the pizza bites are touching. Cook for 12 minutes.
5. Transfer to a plate. Serve warm..

PER SERVING

KILOJOULES: 1531 | **FAT:** 22.8g | **PROTEIN:** 13.1g | **SODIUM:** 987mg
FIBRE: 0.6g | **CARBOHYDRATES:** 18.2g | **SUGAR:** 1.9g

Broccoli Snackers

The slightly browned edges give this sometimes-hated vegetable a new taste and texture.

- **Hands-On Time:** 10 minutes
- **Cook Time:** 12 minutes

Serves 4

1 large head of broccoli, chopped into florets
3/4 tablespoon olive oil
1/2 teaspoon salt

1. Preheat air fryer at 180°C for 3 minutes.
2. In a large bowl, toss broccoli florets with olive oil.
3. Place half of broccoli in fryer basket. Cook for 3 minutes. Shake. Cook for an additional 3 minutes. Transfer to a serving bowl. Season with salt.
4. Repeat with remaining broccoli. Serve warm.

PER SERVING

KILOJOULES: 338 | **FAT:** 3.4g | **PROTEIN:** 4.3g | **SODIUM:** 340mg
FIBRE: 4.0g | **CARBOHYDRATES:** 10.1g | **SUGAR:** 2.6g

Pimiento Cheese-Stuffed Jalapeños

This mild, creamy mixture is great stuffed in spicy jalapeño boats. Because the chillies are seeded, most of the heat is removed. If you like things spicy, mix the seeds in with the pimiento cheese to heat things up.

- **Hands-On Time:** 10 minutes
- **Cook Time:** 16 minutes

Serves 4

6 medium jalapeño chillies
½ cup pimiento cheese

HOW TO MAKE PIMIENTO CHEESE

It's easy! Combine the following ingredients and then refrigerate covered until ready to use: 450 grams finely shredded Cheddar cheese, 110 gram jar diced pimientos including juice, ½ cup mayonnaise, ¼ teaspoon salt and ¼ teaspoon freshly ground black pepper. Stir. Refrigerate for 15 minutes. (If you have trouble finding pimientos in the supermarket, simply substitute with a jar of roasted piquillo peppers or roasted red capsicum.)

1. Cut jalapeño peppers lengthwise and discard seeds. (If you like the heat, stir the seeds into the pimiento cheese.)
2. Press equal amounts pimiento cheese into each jalapeño half.
3. Preheat air fryer at 180°C for 3 minutes.
4. Lay six stuffed peppers into air fryer basket. Cook for 8 minutes. Transfer cooked peppers to a serving plate. Repeat with remaining peppers.
5. Transfer to a serving plate and serve warm.

PER SERVING

KILOJOULES: 71 | **FAT:** 5.2g | **PROTEIN:** 4.1g | **SODIUM:** 160mg | **FIBRE:** 0.6g | **CARBOHYDRATES:** 1.7g | **SUGAR:** 1.0g

Bite-Sized Pork Spring Rolls

These may be a bit tedious to make, but the result is worth it. One way to cut hands-on time is by purchasing already-shredded cabbage and carrots. These are usually labelled "coleslaw mix" and can be found next to the packaged salads in the produce section.

- **Hands-On Time:** 30 minutes
- **Cook Time:** 24 minutes

Serves 10

230 grams lean pork mince
2 cups coleslaw mix (shredded cabbage and carrots)
3 spring onions, trimmed and minced
3/4 tablespoon hoisin sauce
3/4 tablespoon soy sauce
1/4 teaspoon sriracha
1/2 teaspoon lime juice
30 wonton wrappers
2 teaspoons olive oil

SLIMMED-DOWN SPRING ROLLS

If you are counting kilojoules, substitute the pork with turkey mince or chicken mince. The spring rolls will still be fabulous. Other fillings that can be added are sprouts, canned bamboo shoots and shiitake mushrooms.

1. In a large frying pan, heat pork mince over medium-high heat. Stir-fry for 5–6 minutes until no longer pink. Add coleslaw mix and stir into pork. Add spring onions, hoisin sauce, soy sauce, sriracha and lime juice. Stir-fry for an additional 2 minutes. Remove from heat and let rest for 5 minutes off the burner.
2. Place a wonton wrapper on a cutting board. Place a small bowl of water near the board. Spoon approximately 2 teaspoons mixture in a line in the middle of the wrapper. Dip your finger into the water and lightly run it around the perimeter of the wonton wrapper. Fold 5mm of the perimeter of wonton toward the middle. Roll up the length to form a spring roll. Repeat for each wonton wrapper.
3. Preheat air fryer at 160°C for 3 minutes.
4. Place half of the spring rolls in the air fryer basket. Cook for 3 minutes. Lightly brush the tops of spring rolls with olive oil. Cook for an additional 5 minutes. Repeat with second batch.
5. Transfer to a plate. Serve warm.

PER SERVING

KILOJOULES: 443 | **FAT:** 1.2g | **PROTEIN:** 7.5g | **SODIUM:** 268mg
FIBRE: 0.9g | **CARBOHYDRATES:** 15.7g | **SUGAR:** 1.0g

Reuben Pizza for One

If you are a Reuben lover, then this is your pizza. With all of the flavours from the classic Reuben sandwich, it'll ensure that you never want your pizza any other way.

- **Hands-On Time:** 10 minutes
- **Cook Time:** 17 minutes

Makes 1 personal pizza

110 grams fresh pizza dough, about the size of a tennis ball
¼ teaspoon caraway seeds
1 ½ tablespoons Thousand Island dressing (or Russian dressing)
¼ cup chopped corned beef
¼ cup grated Swiss cheese
¼ cup sauerkraut, drained

1 Preheat air fryer at 95°C for 6 minutes.

2 Press out dough to fit pizza pan (accessory). Sprinkle caraway seeds evenly over dough. Cook for 7 minutes.

3 Turn up the heat to 140°C.

4 Remove basket and spread dressing over dough, leaving 6mm outer crust uncovered. Evenly add corned beef. Sprinkle cheese over meat. Cook for an additional 10 minutes.

5 Gently transfer pizza to a cutting board. Evenly add sauerkraut. Cut into six slices and serve.

PER SERVING

KILOJOULES: 3548 | **FAT:** 42.5g | **PROTEIN:** 41.3g | **SODIUM:** 2,409mg
FIBRE: 3.1g | **CARBOHYDRATES:** 62.7g | **SUGAR:** 12.8g

Salmon Croquettes

Traditionally, croquettes are a fried delicacy, as the word *croquette* comes from the French word *croquer*, which means "to crunch" or "to be crunchy". With the air fryer, however, you'll get all the crispness without the unhealthy cooking style. Serve these with your favourite dipping sauce.

- **Hands-On Time:** 15 minutes
- **Cook Time:** 24 minutes

Serves 4

420 grams canned wild-caught salmon, drained
1/3 cup mayonnaise
3/4 tablespoon minced celery
2 teaspoons dried dill, divided
1 teaspoon lime juice
1/2 cup panko bread crumbs, divided
1 large egg
1 teaspoon prepared horseradish
1/4 cup polenta
1 teaspoon salt

1. In a medium bowl, combine salmon, mayonnaise, celery, 1 teaspoon dill, lime juice, 1/4 cup bread crumbs, egg and horseradish.
2. In a shallow dish, combine 1/4 cup bread crumbs, cornmeal, remaining dill and salt.
3. Preheat air fryer at 190°C for 3 minutes.
4. Form 1 1/2 tablespoons salmon mixture into 16 tots or egg shapes. Roll in bread crumb mixture. Continue with remainder of salmon.
5. Place eight tots in lightly greased air fryer basket. Cook for 4 minutes. Gently turn tots a third of the way around. Cook for an additional 4 minutes. Gently turn tots another third. Cook for an additional 4 minutes. Transfer to a serving dish. Repeat with remaining tots. Let rest for 5 minutes before serving warm.

PER SERVING

KILOJOULES: 1652 | **FAT:** 20.1g | **PROTEIN:** 31.6g | **SODIUM:** 1,154mg
FIBRE: 0.5g | **CARBOHYDRATES:** 18.6g | **SUGAR:** 1.0g

Five Spice Crunchy Edamame

The sweet flavour of the edamame pairs nicely with the spices in Chinese five spice. Crispy on the outside and slightly tender on the inside, these snackable bites deliver a healthy dose of fibre, vitamins and minerals.

- **Hands-On Time:** 5 minutes
- **Cook Time:** 16 minutes

Serves 4

1 cup ready-to-eat edamame, shelled
3/4 tablespoon sesame oil
1 teaspoon five spice powder
1/2 teaspoon salt

1. Preheat air fryer at 180°C for 3 minutes.
2. In a small bowl, toss edamame in sesame oil. Add to fryer basket.
3. Place in air fryer basket and cook for 5 minutes. Shake. Cook for an additional 5 minutes. Shake. Cook for an additional 6 minutes.
4. Transfer to a small bowl and toss with five spice powder and salt. Let cool and serve.

PER SERVING

KILOJOULES: 322 | **FAT:** 4.8g | **PROTEIN:** 4.2g | **SODIUM:** 292mg
FIBRE: 2.0g | **CARBOHYDRATES:** 3.9g | **SUGAR:** 0.8g

BBQ Cauliflower Bites

The flavour of this dish can change depending on which barbecue sauce you choose — spicy or sweet. The cauliflower takes on the flavour of whatever you pair it with, all the while delivering your body a healthy punch of vitamin C!

- **Hands-On Time:** 10 minutes
- **Cook Time:** 12 minutes

Serves 4

1 large head cauliflower, chopped into florets, core removed
2 teaspoons olive oil
1/4 cup barbecue sauce of your choice

1. Preheat air fryer at 180°C for 3 minutes.
2. In a large bowl, toss cauliflower florets with olive oil.
3. Place half of cauliflower in fryer basket. Cook for 3 minutes. Shake. Cook for an additional 3 minutes.
4. Transfer to a medium bowl and toss with half the barbecue sauce. Repeat with remaining cauliflower.
5. Transfer to a serving bowl and serve warm.

PER SERVING

KILOJOULES: 426 | **FAT:** 2.6 g | **PROTEIN:** 4.2 g |
SODIUM: 246mg | **FIBRE:** 4.4g | **CARBOHYDRATES:** 17.7g |
SUGAR: 10.0g

Goat Cheese and Prosciutto-Stuffed Mushrooms

Your taste buds will applaud once they taste the creamy goat cheese mixed with the saltiness of the prosciutto, all stuffed in earthy mushrooms. The combination is explosive and the preparation is so simple.

- **Hands-On Time:** 10 minutes
- **Cook Time:** 20 minutes

Serves 4

1/4 cup goat cheese, crumbled
3/4 tablespoon onion, finely chopped
1 teaspoon lemon juice
1/2 teaspoon salt
1/2 teaspoon freshly ground black pepper
450 grams cremini mushrooms, stems removed
1 1/2 tablespoons panko bread crumbs
1 1/2 tablespoons butter, melted
56 grams prosciutto, torn into small pieces
1/4 cup julienned fresh basil

1. In a medium bowl, combine goat cheese, onion, lemon juice, salt and pepper.
2. Preheat air fryer at 180°C for 3 minutes.
3. Evenly stuff goat cheese mixture into mushroom caps. Distribute bread crumbs over stuffed mushrooms. Slowly pour melted butter over bread crumbs.
4. Place half of mushrooms in fryer basket. Cook for 10 minutes. Transfer to serving plate. Repeat with remaining mushrooms.
5. Sprinkle with prosciutto and basil. Serve warm.

PER SERVING

KILOJOULES: 426 | **FAT:** 2.6g | **PROTEIN:** 4.2g | **SODIUM:** 246mg
FIBRE: 4.4g | **CARBOHYDRATES:** 17.9g | **SUGAR:** 10.0g

WHAT IS JULIENNED?

To julienne is simply to cut something into thin, uniform matchsticks. A sharp knife is key to creating clean cuts. Most mandolines also have a julienne function, which makes life much easier when trying to achieve consistently thin vegetables.

Lamb Meatball Gyros

Gyros are traditionally made with meat cooked on a vertical rotisserie, but most of us don't own one. By using meatballs as an alternative, you still get the flavours of the classic without any of the mess.

- **Hands-On Time:** 15 minutes
- **Cook Time:** 8 minutes

Serves 4

230 grams lamb mince
1/2 cup plain bread crumbs
1 teaspoon chopped fresh mint
1/4 teaspoon ground coriander
2 cloves garlic, minced
1 teaspoon salt
2 pita rounds
2 medium Roma tomatoes, seeded and diced
1/4 cup diced red onion
1/4 cup Tzatziki Sauce (see page 75)

1. Preheat air fryer at 180°C for 3 minutes.
2. In a medium bowl, combine lamb, bread crumbs, mint, coriander, garlic and salt. Form into eight meatballs, about 2 tablespoons each.
3. Add meatballs to fryer basket and cook for 6 minutes. Flip meatballs. Cook for an additional 2 minutes. Transfer to a plate.
4. Open pita rounds and add half the meatballs to each. Add half the tomatoes, red onion and tzatziki sauce to each and serve.

PER SERVING

KILOJOULES: 2351 | **FAT:** 19.4g | **PROTEIN:** 34.4g | **SODIUM:** 1,881mg | **FIBRE:** 2.8g | **CARBOHYDRATES:** 55.3g | **SUGAR:** 3.6g

HOW DO YOU PRONOUNCE "GYRO"?

Many people say JAI-roh, so because you subscribe to a sort of groupthink and don't want to sound snooty, you'll pronounce it that way, too. Who cares? But, really, don't you secretly want to know how to say it correctly? One gyro is pronounced YEE-roh, and two or more gyri are pronounced YEE-ree.

Pork Meatball Banh Mi

A banh mi, a Vietnamese sandwich, is made a hundred different ways, but the basics are a baguette, meat, vegetables and a sauce. The recipe has a long list of ingredients, but use them all. There is a balance achieved by using every one.

- **Hands-On Time:** 15 minutes
- **Cook Time:** 9 minutes

Serves 2

1/4 cup rice vinegar
1/8 cup water
1/8 cup honey
1 large carrot, peeled and shredded
6 medium radishes, julienned
1 1/2 tablespoons diced white onion
1/4 cup julienned cucumbers
230 grams lean pork mince
1/2 teaspoon ground ginger
1/2 teaspoon ground cumin
1 teaspoon fish sauce
1 teaspoon soy sauce
1/2 cup plain bread crumbs
1 (30cm) French baguette, cut crosswise into 2 (15cm) sections
1/2 cup shredded iceberg lettuce
1/4 cup Sriracha Mayonnaise (see page 72)

SHOULD I SKIP FISH SAUCE?

No. Fish sauce might sound gross when it is defined as fermented anchovy juice. But fish sauce provides the umami (taste sensation) that brings the flavours together. Use it as a salt substitute in stir-fries and other Asian dishes.

1. In a small saucepan over medium-high heat, heat vinegar, water and honey for 1 minute. Set aside for 5 minutes.
2. Place carrot, radishes, onion and cucumbers in a medium bowl and pour vinegar sauce over them to pickle them. Refrigerate covered for 30 minutes or until ready to use. Strain.
3. Preheat air fryer at 180°C for 3 minutes.
4. Combine pork, ginger, cumin, fish sauce, soy sauce and bread crumbs. Form into eight meatballs, about 2 tablespoons each.
5. Add meatballs to fryer basket and cook for 6 minutes. Flip meatballs. Cook for an additional 2 minutes. Transfer to a plate.
6. Slice baguettes lengthwise and add four meatballs to each. Top with pickled vegetables and lettuce. Drizzle each sandwich with half the sriracha mayonnaise. Serve immediately

PER SERVING

KILOJOULES: 2343 | **FAT:** 24.6g | **PROTEIN:** 23,3g | **SODIUM:** 1,248mg | **FIBRE:** 4.4g | **CARBOHYDRATES:** 58.4g | **SUGAR:** 9.9g

Lobster Rolls

This trendy pub classic can be yours in minutes. The lobster meat shines with very little seasoning. Traditionally served on a top-slit buttered hot dog bun, the lobster salad is great on its own or even in a lettuce wrap!

- **Hands-On Time:** 15 minutes
- **Cook Time:** 10 minutes

Serves 2

2 (140-170 gram) small uncooked lobster tails
2 1/4 tablespoons butter, melted, divided
1 1/2 tablespoons mayonnaise
1 small stalk celery, diced
2 teaspoons fresh lemon juice
1/2 teaspoon fresh lemon zest
1/4 teaspoon smoked paprika
1/4 teaspoon salt
1/8 teaspoon freshly ground black pepper
2 top-split buns
1/2 cup shredded lettuce

HOW TO SHRED LETTUCE

Simply take a cleaned head of iceberg lettuce and give it a quick pound, stem-side down, on your kitchen bench. This will allow you to easily remove and discard the core. Cut the remaining lettuce in quarters and then grate on the large holes of a box grater.

1. Using kitchen shears, cut down the middle of the lobster tail on the softer side. Carefully run your finger between the lobster meat and the shell to loosen meat.
2. Preheat air fryer at 200°C for 3 minutes.
3. Place tails in air fryer basket, cut side up. Cook for 4 minutes. Brush with 1 tablespoon butter. Cook for an additional 3–4 minutes, depending on the size of the lobster tail.
4. Roughly chop lobster meat and transfer to a medium bowl. Combine lobster with mayonnaise, celery, lemon juice, lemon zest, paprika, salt and pepper. Refrigerate covered until ready to use.
5. Brush remaining butter on each inner side of the buns. Cook for 1–2 minutes at 200°C in air fryer.
6. Distribute lobster mixture and lettuce between the buns and serve.

PER SERVING

KILOJOULES: 2045 | **FAT:** 28.8g | **PROTEIN:** 30.6g | **SODIUM:** 1,266mg | **FIBRE:** 1.6g | **CARBOHYDRATES:** 23.0g | **SUGAR:** 3.6g

Fried Peanut Butter and Banana Sandwiches

Peanut butter and banana make a wonderful combination. With the addition of honey and then air frying the sandwich, the extra sweetness and crunchy sandwich bread almost makes this a dessert.

- **Hands-On Time:** 10 minutes
- **Cook Time:** 12 minutes

Serves 2

1 1/2 tablespoons smooth peanut butter

4 slices white sandwich bread

1 large banana, sliced

2 teaspoons honey

1 1/2 tablespoons butter, melted

1 Spread peanut butter on one side of 2 slices of bread. Layer each with sliced bananas and drizzle each with honey. Top with remaining bread.

2 Preheat air fryer at 180°C for 3 minutes.

3 Brush the outside top and bottom of a sandwich lightly with melted butter. Place in air fryer basket one at a time and cook for 3 minutes. Flip and cook for an additional 3 minutes.

4 Repeat with other sandwich. Serve warm.

PER SERVING

KILOJOULES: 1723 | **FAT:** 17.7g | **PROTEIN:** 9.7g | **SODIUM:** 298mg
FIBRE: 4.2g | **CARBOHYDRATES:** 54.6g | **SUGAR:** 19.2g

WHY IS SOME HONEY RUNNY AND SOME THICKER?

All honey is actually in a liquid state when jarred; however, raw honey isn't filtered, so the pollen and beeswax are still present. It goes through a natural crystallisation state, causing it to harden a bit in the jar. The type of flower from which the bee gets its nectar determines how fast the honey hardens. Runny honey has been filtered and heated, so the hardening quality is diminished but it is easier to use quickly in everyday recipes.

Chicken Parmesan Grilled Cheese Sandwich

What happens when two sought-after foods collide? This sandwich! Although the napoletana sauce can be used out of a jar, if you take the time to prepare the Spicy Napoletana Sauce (see recipe on page 70), the results will be much appreciated.

- **Hands-On Time:** 10 minutes
- **Cook Time:** 12 minutes

Serves 2

1 ½ tablespoons Spicy Napoletana Sauce (see page 70)
4 slices sourdough bread
1 ½ tablespoons grated Parmesan cheese
½ cup chopped cooked chicken
4 slices fresh mozzarella cheese
1 ½ tablespoons butter, melted

1. Spread napoletana sauce on one side of 2 slices of bread. Sprinkle with Parmesan cheese. Layer with chicken and mozzarella slices. Top each with remaining slices of bread.
2. Preheat air fryer at 180°C for 3 minutes.
3. Brush the outside top and bottom of a sandwich lightly with melted butter. Place in air fryer basket one at a time and cook for 3 minutes. Flip and cook for an additional 3 minutes.
4. Repeat with other sandwich. Serve warm.

PER SERVING

KILOJOULES: 2736 | **FAT:** 25.1g | **PROTEIN:** 38.1g | **SODIUM:** 1,203mg | **FIBRE:** 2.8g | **CARBOHYDRATES:** 62.0g | **SUGAR:** 6.5g

Brie, Fig and Prosciutto Open-Faced Sandwiches

Sweet, salty and creamy, these open-faced sandwiches hit all the yummy buttons. Serve on regular-sized bread for a meal for two or prepare these as appetisers on smaller sliced French bread for some happy partygoers.

- **Hands-On Time:** 5 minutes
- **Cook Time:** 4 minutes

Serves 2

1/4 cup Brie cheese
1/4 cup fig jam
2 slices ciabatta bread (or other crusty artisanal bread)
1/2 cup rocket, stems removed
4 slices prosciutto, ripped into big, rustic pieces
1/2 teaspoon olive oil

1. Preheat air fryer at 180°C for 3 minutes.
2. Spread a layer of Brie and then fig jam on each slice of bread.
3. Place topped bread in air fryer basket. Cook for 3–4 minutes until cheese is melty and warm.
4. Top each sandwich with rocket and prosciutto pieces. Lightly drizzle 1/4 teaspoon olive oil on each sandwich. Serve warm.

PER SERVING

KILOJOULES: 1748 | **FAT:** 13.2g | **PROTEIN:** 16.1g | **SODIUM:** 580mg | **FIBRE:** 1.8g | **CARBOHYDRATES:** 57.9g | **SUGAR:** 22.2g

WHAT IS ROCKET?

Rocket is a leafy green that you should be eating. Because of its tangy and natural peppery flavour, it is especially good on sandwiches. A great source of antioxidants and vitamin K, rocket is also high in some B vitamins, which are known to increase your metabolism.

Grilled Cheese Croutons

An unexpected pop of cheese is always welcomed. Float these croutons on a bowl of soup or salad. Try complementary cheeses in this recipe for a bumped-up experience each time. Pssst ... fetta croutons are amazing on a fresh Greek salad!

- **Hands-On Time:** 10 minutes
- **Cook Time:** 12 minutes

Serves 2

2 slices Cheddar cheese
2 slices provolone cheese
4 slices sourdough bread
1 ½ tablespoons butter, melted

1 Place 1 slice of Cheddar cheese and 1 slice of provolone cheese between 2 pieces of bread. Repeat.

2 Preheat air fryer at 180°C for 3 minutes.

3 Brush the outside top and bottom of each sandwich lightly with melted butter. Place in air fryer basket one at a time and cook for 3 minutes. Transfer sandwich to a clean, flat surface. Gently press sandwich flat with a heavy, flat pan or frying pan. Add sandwich back to air fryer basket and cook for an additional 3 minutes. Repeat with second sandwich.

4 Cut sandwiches into 3cm cubes and serve.

PER SERVING

KILOJOULES: 2502 | **FAT:** 25.4g | **PROTEIN:** 26.3g | **SODIUM:** 1,114mg | **FIBRE:** 2.5g | **CARBOHYDRATES:** 59.8g | **SUGAR:** 5.5g

California Turkey Sandwiches

The avocado, tomato and sprouts give this sandwich its California name. But the turkey and rosemary mayonnaise give a little nod to the holidays, creating a unique combination of tasty! If you don't have Gruyère, substitute Swiss cheese, as it is the closest in taste.

- **Hands-On Time:** 10 minutes
- **Cook Time:** 12 minutes

Serves 2

1 1/2 tablespoons Rosemary Mayonnaise (see page 69)
4 slices ciabatta bread (or other crusty artisanal bread)
110 grams thinly sliced deli turkey
110 grams thinly sliced Gruyère cheese
1 small avocado, peeled, pitted and sliced
1 medium Roma tomato, thinly sliced
1/2 cup alfalfa sprouts
1 1/2 tablespoons butter, melted

1. Spread rosemary mayonnaise on inside of each piece of bread.
2. Build sandwiches between bread slices by evenly distributing turkey, Gruyère cheese, avocado, tomato and sprouts.
3. Preheat air fryer at 180°C for 3 minutes.
4. Brush the outside top and bottom of a sandwich lightly with melted butter. Place in air fryer basket and cook for 3 minutes. Flip and cook for an additional 3 minutes.
5. Repeat with other sandwich. Serve warm.

PER SERVING

KILOJOULES: 3740 | **FAT:** 49.0g | **PROTEIN:** 36.7g | **SODIUM:** 1,923mg | **FIBRE:** 8.5g | **CARBOHYDRATES:** 68.7g | **SUGAR:** 4.6g

TYPES OF SPROUTS

Sprouts are the germinating shoots of seeds. They are not only edible but are incredibly nutritious. In recent years, supermarkets have been offering more than alfalfa and bean sprouts. Broccoli sprouts, radish sprouts and lentil sprouts are also showing up. Because of the pricey tag, many people grow their own!

Personal Pepperoni and Mushroom Pizza

This recipe is for one, with the suggestion of adding pepperoni and mushrooms. However, you can double or quadruple this recipe and get family members involved in adding their favourite toppings to their individual pizzas.

- **Hands-On Time:** 10 minutes
- **Cook Time:** 17 minutes

Makes 1 personal pizza

110 grams fresh pizza dough, about the size of a tennis ball

1 ½ tablespoons napoletana or pizza sauce

6 slices pepperoni

¼ cup sliced white mushrooms

¼ cup grated mozzarella cheese

1. Preheat air fryer at 95°C for 6 minutes.
2. Press out dough to fit pizza pan (accessory). Cook for 7 minutes.
3. Turn up the heat to 140°C. Remove basket and spread sauce over dough, leaving 6mm outer crust uncovered. Add pepperoni slices and mushrooms. Sprinkle cheese over both. Cook for an additional 10 minutes.
4. Gently transfer pizza to a cutting board. Cut into six slices and serve.

PER SERVING

KILOJOULES: 2317 | **FAT:** 16.3g | **PROTEIN:** 21.9g | **SODIUM:** 2,154mg | **FIBRE:** 6.7g | **CARBOHYDRATES:** 75.1g | **SUGAR:** 22.1g

5

Sauces and Dips

Cocktail Sauce

Home chefs sometimes only mix together tomato sauce and horseradish. Take the time to add all the ingredients, as they lend depth of flavour and give balance to your sauce.

- **Hands-On Time:** 5 minutes
- **Cook Time:** 0 minutes

Makes approximately 1¼ cups

1 cup tomato sauce
1 ½ tablespoons prepared horseradish
¾ tablespoon lemon juice
½ teaspoon Worcestershire sauce
⅛ teaspoon Tabasco sauce
⅛ teaspoon chilli powder
¼ teaspoon salt
Pinch freshly ground black pepper

1 Combine ingredients in a small bowl and refrigerate covered until ready to use, for up to 1 week.

PER SERVING (2 TABLESPOONS)

KILOJOULES: 108 | FAT: 0.0g | PROTEIN: 0.3g | SODIUM: 292mg | FIBRE: 0.2g | CARBOHYDRATES: 7.1g | SUGAR: 5.4g

Blue Cheese Dipping Sauce

Tangy and sharp in taste, the fresh blue cheese crumbles in this homemade version make it superior to the products found on shelves. Also terrific drizzled over a fresh steak salad!

- **Hands-On Time:** 10 minutes
- **Cook Time:** 0 minutes

Makes approximately 1½ cups

1 cup crumbled blue cheese
½ cup mayonnaise
½ cup plain Greek yoghurt
¾ tablespoon full-cream milk
¼ cup chopped fresh parsley
½ teaspoon salt
¼ teaspoon freshly ground black pepper

1 Combine all the ingredients in a small bowl and refrigerate covered until ready to use, for up to 1 week.

PER SERVING (2 TABLESPOONS)

KILOJOULES: 468 | FAT: 10.3g | PROTEIN: 3.4g | SODIUM: 288mg | FIBRE: 0.1g | CARBOHYDRATES: 0.9g | SUGAR: 0.6g

Basic Honey Mustard Sauce

This sauce is terrific with air-fried vegetables or chicken bites, as a salad dressing and even on tacos. Whisk in a little barbecue sauce to make honey BBQ sauce!

- **Hands-On Time:** 5 minutes
- **Cook Time:** 0 minutes

Makes approximately 3/4 cups

1/4 cup honey
1/4 cup yellow mustard
1/8 cup mayonnaise
3/4 tablespoon apple cider vinegar
1 teaspoon freshly ground black pepper

1 Combine all the ingredients in a small bowl and refrigerate covered until ready to use, for up to 1 week.

PER SERVING (2 TABLESPOONS)

KILOJOULES: 338 | **FAT:** 3.7g | **PROTEIN:** 0.5g | **SODIUM:** 144mg | **FIBRE:** 0.5g | **CARBOHYDRATES:** 12.5g | **SUGAR:** 11.7g

Tartar Sauce

Tartar sauce is a mayonnaise-based sauce traditionally served with fried seafood. It's also good on seafood tacos. There are many who also swear by dipping the ever-humble French fry in it, so give it a try!

- **Hands-On Time:** 5 minutes
- **Cook Time:** 0 minutes

Makes approximately 1 cups

1/2 cup mayonnaise
3/4 tablespoon Dijon mustard
1/2 cup small-diced dill pickles
Pinch salt
1/4 teaspoon freshly ground black pepper

1 Combine all the ingredients in a small bowl and refrigerate covered until ready to use, for up to 1 week.

PER SERVING (2 TABLESPOONS)

KILOJOULES: 410 | **FAT:** 10.3g | **PROTEIN:** 0.3g | **SODIUM:** 224mg | **FIBRE:** 0.1g | **CARBOHYDRATES:** 0.94g | **SUGAR:** 0.2g

Napoletana Sauce

One of the tastiest and most versatile tomato-based sauces out there, napoletana sauce is perfect for pasta, fried eggplant, mozzarella and a classic parmigiana.

- **Hands-On Time:** 10 minutes
- **Cook Time:** 30 minutes

Makes 4 cups

800 grams canned crushed tomatoes, including juice
1 medium stalk celery, finely diced
1 medium carrot, peeled and finely diced
1/2 medium red onion, peeled and finely diced
4 cloves garlic, quartered
1 1/2 tablespoons chopped fresh basil
1 1/2 tablespoons chopped fresh Italian flat-leaf parsley
3/4 tablespoon fresh thyme leaves
1 teaspoon sea salt
1/2 teaspoon freshly ground black pepper
1/2 cup beef broth

1 Combine all ingredients in a large heavy-bottomed pot over high heat. Bring to a boil. Reduce heat and simmer covered for 30 minutes.

2 Use an immersion blender to blend the sauce in the pot until smooth. Let cool.

3 Pour the sauce into an air tight container or jar and refrigerate until ready to use. Use within 5 days.

PER SERVING (1/2 CUP)

KILOJOULES: 175 | **FAT:** 0.3g | **PROTEIN:** 2.2g | **SODIUM:** 445mg | **FIBRE:** 2.5g | **CARBOHYDRATES:** 9.5g | **SUGAR:** 5.1g

Tomato Curry Sauce

This creamy dairy-free sauce is excellent served over cauliflower "rice", seafood, chicken and even your breakfast eggs! Full of flavour and Indian spices, this recipe is heavenly.

- **Hands-On Time:** 10 minutes
- **Cook Time:** 15 minutes

Makes 2 cups

410 grams can crushed tomatoes, including juice
1 1/2 tablespoons minced onion
2 cloves garlic, quartered
1 teaspoon ground ginger
1/4 teaspoon garam masala
1/4 teaspoon ground turmeric
1/8 teaspoon red pepper flakes
1/8 teaspoon ground cinnamon
2 teaspoons fresh thyme leaves
1/2 teaspoon sea salt
1/4 teaspoon freshly ground black pepper
1/4 cup canned coconut milk

1. Combine all ingredients in a large heavy-bottomed pot or Dutch oven. Bring to a boil over high heat. Reduce heat and simmer covered for 20 minutes.
2. Use an immersion blender to blend the sauce in the pot until smooth.
3. Pour sauce into an airtight container or jar and refrigerate until ready to use. Use within 5 days.

PER SERVING (1/2 CUP)

KILOJOULES: 280 | **FAT:** 3.1g | **PROTEIN:** 2.2g | **SODIUM:** 483mg | **FIBRE:** 2.3g | **CARBOHYDRATES:** 9.6g | **SUGAR:** 4.8g

WHAT IS COCONUT MILK?

Coconut milk is simply coconut meat and coconut water. That's it! Be mindful of labels when purchasing coconut milk, as some brands add emulsifiers and fillers. You should be able to easily buy canned versions from reputable companies. Stay away from the "light" varieties, as this takes away from the natural healthy fats found in coconut and is counter to the whole-food mentality.

Pico Guacamole

Pico guacamole is the baby from the marriage of salsa and guacamole. When dicing the avocado, be sure to immediately toss the cubes in the lime juice to avoid browning. Serve over scrambled eggs, with tacos or as a dip with air fried tortilla chips.

- **Hands-On Time:** 10 minutes
- **Cook Time:** 0 minutes

Makes approximately 1 cup

Juice of 1 small lime
2 medium avocados, peeled, pitted and diced
4 cloves garlic, minced
1 teaspoon sriracha
1 teaspoon sea salt
¼ cup chopped fresh coriander
2 medium Roma tomatoes, seeded and diced

1 Combine lime juice and diced avocado in a small bowl. Using the back of a fork, press avocado so it is half smooshed. Stir in remaining ingredients.

2 Serve immediately. Cover and refrigerate any leftovers (to avoid browning) for up to 3 days.

PER SERVING (2 TABLESPOONS)

KILOJOULES: 263 | **FAT:** 4.7g | **PROTEIN:** 0.9g | **SODIUM:** 211mg | **FIBRE:** 2.6g | **CARBOHYDRATES:** 4.5g | **SUGAR:** 0.7g

Rosemary Mayonnaise

Rosemary is an herb that makes this an ideal mayonnaise to use in a turkey sandwich. It's also good with BBQ prawns, sweet-potato fries and even slathered on a beef or turkey burger!

- **Hands-On Time:** 5 minutes
- **Cook Time:** 0 minutes

Makes 1/2 cup

1/2 cup mayonnaise
3/4 tablespoon finely chopped fresh rosemary
1/2 teaspoon fresh lemon juice
1/2 teaspoon fresh lemon zest
1/4 teaspoon sea salt
1/8 teaspoon cayenne pepper

1 Combine all the ingredients in a small bowl and refrigerate covered until ready to use, for up to 1 week.

PER SERVING (2 TABLESPOONS)

KILOJOULES: 782 | **FAT:** 20.2g | **PROTEIN:** 0.3g | **SODIUM:** 272mg | **FIBRE:** 0.1g | **CARBOHYDRATES:** 0.4g | **SUGAR:** 0.2g

Spicy Napoletana Sauce

If you like a little heat with your napoletana, add some red chilli flakes to this sauce to kick it up a notch. Taste as you go to hit the level that you can handle.

- **Hands-On Time:** 10 minutes
- **Cook Time:** 30 minutes

Makes 4 cups

800 grams canned crushed tomatoes, including juice

1 medium carrot, peeled and finely diced

1/2 medium red onion, peeled and finely diced

4 cloves garlic, quartered

1/2 teaspoon red chilli flakes

3/4 tablespoon balsamic vinegar

1 1/2 tablespoons chopped fresh basil

1 1/2 tablespoons chopped fresh Italian flat-leaf parsley

1 teaspoon sea salt

1/2 teaspoon freshly ground black pepper

1/2 cup beef broth

1. Combine all ingredients in a large heavy-bottomed pot over high heat. Bring to a boil. Reduce heat and simmer covered for 30 minutes.
2. Use an immersion blender to blend the sauce in the pot until smooth. Let cool.
3. Pour the sauce into an airtight container or jar and refrigerate until ready to use. Use within 5 days.

PER SERVING (1/2 CUP)

KILOJOULES: 179 | **FAT:** 0.3g | **PROTEIN:** 2.1g | **SODIUM:** 441mg | **FIBRE:** 2.3g | **CARBOHYDRATES:** 9.6g | **SUGAR:** 5.3g

Super Easy Romesco Sauce

This roasted capsicum and almond-based sauce can be stirred into pasta, spread on sandwiches and also used as a dip for a crudités tray.

- **Hands-On Time:** 5 minutes
- **Cook Time:** 5 minutes

Makes approximately 2 cups

340 grams jar roasted red capsicum, drained
28 gram slice ciabatta bread, cubed
1/4 cup diced tomatoes, drained
1/3 cup chopped fresh parsley
2 cloves garlic, halved
1/2 cup chopped almonds
1/4 cup olive oil
3/4 tablespoon cooking sherry
1/2 teaspoon smoked paprika
2 teaspoons sriracha
1/2 teaspoon salt
1/4 teaspoon freshly ground black pepper

1. In a medium saucepan, add all ingredients and heat over medium heat for 5 minutes, stirring occasionally.
2. Use an immersion blender to blend the sauce in the saucepan until smooth.
3. Pour sauce into an airtight container or jar and refrigerate until ready to use. Use within 5 days.

PER SERVING (2 TABLESPOONS)

KILOJOULES: 238 | **FAT:** 4.8g | **PROTEIN:** 1.1g | **SODIUM:** 390mg | **FIBRE:** 0.8g | **CARBOHYDRATES:** 2.9g | **SUGAR:** 0.4g

Horseradish-Lemon Aioli

In modern terms, aioli has come to mean a flavoured mayonnaise. This horseradish-lemon aioli is delicious paired with crab cakes or fried shrimp or spread on the buns of seafood sliders!

- **Hands-On Time:** 5 minutes
- **Cook Time:** 0 minutes

Makes approximately ¾ cups

½ cup mayonnaise
4 teaspoons prepared horseradish
2 teaspoons fresh lemon zest
¼ teaspoon fresh lemon juice

1 Combine ingredients in a small bowl and refrigerate covered until ready to use, for up to 1 week.

PER SERVING (2 TABLESPOONS)

KILOJOULES: 527 | **FAT:** 13.4g | **PROTEIN:** 0.2g | **SODIUM:** 130mg | **FIBRE:** 0.2g | **CARBOHYDRATES:** 0.6g | **SUGAR:** 0.4g

Sriracha Mayonnaise

If spicy is your thing, just add a squirt or two more of the sriracha. Also, if you are using this for tacos, add the mayonnaise to a squirt bottle for a pretty drizzle on your food. Alternatively, spoon the mayonnaise mixture into a plastic sandwich bag and snip off just the tip of the corner.

- **Hands-On Time:** 5 minutes
- **Cook Time:** 0 minutes

Makes approximately ½ cups

½ cup mayonnaise
2 teaspoons sriracha
1 teaspoon lime juice
Pinch salt

1 Combine all the ingredients in a small bowl and refrigerate covered until ready to use, for up to 1 week.

PER SERVING (2 TABLESPOONS)

KILOJOULES: 790 | **FAT:** 20.1g | **PROTEIN:** 0.3g | **SODIUM:** 260mg | **FIBRE:** 0.0g | **CARBOHYDRATES:** 0.8g | **SUGAR:** 0.7g

Sweet Chilli Sauce

The spices and heat from the sambal oelek is tempered and sweetened by the added sugar, creating an addictive balance in this sauce, which also makes an amazing dip for spring rolls.

- **Hands-On Time:** 10 minutes
- **Cook Time:** 3 minutes

Makes approximately ½ cups

1 ½ tablespoons sambal oelek
4 cloves garlic, halved
1 cup sugar
1 cup rice vinegar
½ teaspoon salt
¾ cup plus ¾ tablespoon water, divided
1 tablespoon cornflour

1. In a medium saucepan, add sambel oelek, garlic, sugar, vinegar, salt and ¾ cup water. Bring to a rolling boil, for 2 minutes.
2. In a small bowl, create a slurry by adding ¾ tablespoon water to the cornflour.
3. Slowly whisk slurry into boiling sauce mixture. Reduce heat and allow to simmer 1 additional minute to thicken. Discard garlic. Allow mixture to cool. Refrigerate covered until ready to use, within 7 days.

PER SERVING (1 TABLESPOONS)

KILOJOULES: 447 | **FAT:** 0.0g | **PROTEIN:** 0.1g | **SODIUM:** 83mg | **FIBRE:** 0.0g | **CARBOHYDRATES:** 26.4g | **SUGAR:** 25.2g

WHAT IS SAMBAL OELEK?

Sambal oelek is an Indonesian chilli paste usually containing salt, vinegar and other spices. It can be found at most supermarkets in the Asian cuisine aisle. It actually has the same ingredients and heat level as sriracha but it has zero sugars, so if you are adhering to a carb-free diet, this is your hot sauce!

Horseradish Sauce

Traditionally served with prime rib, this horseradish sauce also confers its benefits on roast beef sandwiches. Or stir some into room-temperature cream cheese for a raw vegetable dip!

- **Hands-On Time:** 10 minutes
- **Cook Time:** 0 minutes

Makes approximately 1 cup

- 1/4 cup mayonnaise
- 1/4 cup sour cream
- 1/4 cup prepared horseradish, plus more if needed
- 2 teaspoons Dijon mustard
- 3/4 tablespoon lemon juice
- 1/4 teaspoon hot sauce
- 1/2 teaspoon Worcestershire sauce
- 1/2 teaspoon freshly ground black pepper

1. Combine all the ingredients in a small bowl. Taste and add more horseradish for more kick if desired. Refrigerate covered until ready to use, for up to 1 week.

PER SERVING (2 TABLESPOONS)

KILOJOULES: 476 | **FAT:** 11.5g | **PROTEIN:** 0.5g | **SODIUM:** 157mg | **FIBRE:** 0.3g | **CARBOHYDRATES:** 1.5g | **SUGAR:** 1.0g

Hollandaise Sauce

Primarily found served over eggs Benedict, this creamy, dreamy emulsion can also be served over fish cakes, salmon, asparagus and crab dishes.

- **Hands-On Time:** 10 minutes
- **Cook Time:** 5 minutes

Makes approximately 1 1/2 cups

- 4 large egg yolks
- 3/4 tablespoon lemon juice
- 1/2 cup unsalted butter, cut into 8 pats
- Pinch salt
- Pinch cayenne pepper
- Pinch ground white pepper

1. Whisk egg yolks and lemon juice together over a double boiler.
2. Quickly whisk in one pat of butter at a time until all of the butter is used and sauce has thickened. Sprinkle in seasonings. If sauce starts to curdle, add in a little of the hot double-boiler water and whisk. Serve immediately.

PER SERVING (2 TABLESPOONS)

KILOJOULES: 359 | **FAT:** 8.6g | **PROTEIN:** 1.0g | **SODIUM:** 15mg | **FIBRE:** 0.0g | **CARBOHYDRATES:** 0.3g | **SUGAR:** 0.1g

Traditional Pesto

Pesto is a great sauce to make when your garden is overflowing with herbs. Traditionally made with basil and/or parsley, try swapping out herbs for different main dishes. For example, mint pesto is amazing served with lamb kebabs.

- **Hands-On Time:** 5 minutes
- **Cook Time:** 0 minutes

Makes approximately ½ cup

3 cups fresh basil leaves
⅓ cup pine nuts
4 cloves garlic, halved
¾ cup freshly grated Parmesan cheese
3-4 tablespoons olive oil
Pinch salt

1 Pulse basil and pine nuts in a food processor. Add garlic, cheese and 1 tablespoon olive oil. Pulse. Slowly add remaining oil until desired consistency is reached. Add a pinch of salt. Transfer to a jar and refrigerate. Use within 5 days.

PER SERVING (2 TABLESPOONS)

KILOJOULES: 753 | **FAT:** 13.0g | **PROTEIN:** 7.6g | **SODIUM:** 375mg | **FIBRE:** 0.8g | **CARBOHYDRATES:** 5.6g | **SUGAR:** 0.5g

Tzatziki Sauce

This yoghurt-based sauce has a mix of very fresh flavours, such as cucumber, dill, mint and lemon. This sauce is served mostly with Greek dishes, such as gyros, salads and Greek meatballs, also known as keftedes. But it is also a great choice for chicken or fish.

- **Hands-On Time:** 10 minutes
- **Cook Time:** 0 minutes

Makes approximately 2 ½ cups

2 cups plain Greek yoghurt
1 medium English cucumber, peeled and diced small
2 teaspoons chopped fresh dill
2 teaspoons chopped fresh mint
1 teaspoon salt
2 teaspoons lemon juice
3 cloves garlic, minced

1 Combine all the ingredients in a medium bowl and refrigerate covered until ready to use, for up to 1 week.

PER SERVING (2 TABLESPOONS)

KILOJOULES: 96 | **FAT:** 1.1g | **PROTEIN:** 2.1g | **SODIUM:** 124mg | **FIBRE:** 0.1g | **CARBOHYDRATES:** 1.3g | **SUGAR:** 1.1g

Remoulade Special Sauce

Invented in France, this mayonnaise-based sauce is excellent on sandwiches and even as a base in a cold prawn or crab salad. If you want to create umami (taste sensation), finely chop a few anchovies and throw them in.

- **Hands-On Time:** 5 minutes
- **Cook Time:** 0 minutes

Makes approximately 1½ cups

1 cup mayonnaise
¼ cup Dijon mustard
¾ tablespoon sweet paprika
2 teaspoons Cajun seasoning
1 teaspoon lemon juice
¾ tablespoon sweet pickle relish
2 cloves garlic, minced
¾ tablespoon finely chopped fresh parsley
¼ teaspoon hot sauce

1 Combine all the ingredients in a small bowl and refrigerate covered until ready to use, for up to 1 week.

PER SERVING (2 TABLESPOONS)

KILOJOULES: 577 | **FAT:** 14.0g | **PROTEIN:** 0.2g | **SODIUM:** 296mg | **FIBRE:** 0.2g | **CARBOHYDRATES:** 1.3g | **SUGAR:** 0.2g

6

Side Dishes

Disco Fries

Disco fries are similar to poutine, but poutine has gravy over the fries and is topped with cheese curds. These fries traditionally have Cheddar cheese or mozzarella, but this recipe throws in an upscale twist with gravy and some creamy goats cheese.

- **Hands-On Time:** 10 minutes
- **Cook Time:** 18 minutes

Serves 2

2 medium potatoes, scrubbed and cut lengthwise into 6mm fries

2 teaspoons olive oil

3 teaspoons salt, divided

½ cup brown gravy, warmed (see below)

3 tablespoons goat cheese, crumbled

HOW TO MAKE BROWN GRAVY

Brown gravy can be purchased already jarred or made from meat drippings. But what if you aren't cooking meat and still want a homemade version? In a small saucepan over medium-high heat, melt 2 ¼ tablespoons unsalted butter. Whisk in 2 ¼ tablespoons plain flour. Slowly whisk in 1 cup beef broth, 1 teaspoon Worcestershire sauce and ½ teaspoon garlic salt until sauce thickens. If sauce is too thick, add a tablespoon at a time of beef broth or water until desired consistency.

1. Place fries in a medium saucepan. Cover fries with water. Add olive oil and 1 teaspoon salt. Bring to a boil. Boil for 3 minutes until fork-tender but still somewhat firm. Drain.
2. Preheat air fryer at 200°C for 3 minutes.
3. Toss fries with 1 teaspoon salt. Place fries in fryer basket and cook for 5 minutes. Shake basket. Cook for an additional 5 minutes. Shake. Season with remaining teaspoon salt. Cook for an additional 5 minutes.
4. Transfer to a plate and top with gravy and crumbled goat cheese. Serve warm.

PER SERVING

KILOJOULES: 974 | **FAT:** 8.9g | **PROTEIN:** 6.6g | **SODIUM:** 2,979mg | **FIBRE:** 2.7g | **CARBOHYDRATES:** 30.4g | **SUGAR:** 2.2g

Baked Potatoes

The air fryer can cook the potatoes much faster than your oven. Although a microwave can achieve this cook in an even shorter time, the air fryer crisps up the outer skin while cooking the centre to perfection!

- **Hands-On Time:** 5 minutes
- **Cook Time:** 45 minutes

Serves 2

2 large potatoes (about 450 grams), scrubbed

2 teaspoons olive oil

1 ½ tablespoons butter, cut into 2 pats

½ teaspoon salt

¼ teaspoon freshly ground black pepper

1. Preheat air fryer at 200°C for 3 minutes.
2. Rub olive oil over both potatoes. Place in air fryer basket.
3. Cook for 30 minutes. Flip potatoes. Cook for an additional 15 minutes.
4. Once cooled, slice each potato lengthwise about 1cm deep. Pinch ends to open up slice. Add a pat of butter and season with salt and pepper. Serve warm.

PER SERVING

KILOJOULES: 1753 | **FAT:** 15.3g | **PROTEIN:** 7.6g | **SODIUM:** 1,606mg | **FIBRE:** 6.7g | **CARBOHYDRATES:** 63.4g | **SUGAR:** 3.5g

Roasted Garlic Mashed Potatoes

The skins of the potatoes not only add nutrition to your mashed potatoes, but also contribute to the texture and rustic flavour of the dish.

- **Hands-On Time:** 10 minutes
- **Cook Time:** 14 minutes

Serves 4

450 grams Yukon Gold potatoes (2 medium), scrubbed and diced into 3cm cubes

3 cloves garlic, halved

1 1/2 tablespoons butter, melted

1/2 teaspoon salt

1/2 teaspoon freshly ground black pepper

1/4 cup thickened cream

1 tablespoon butter (not melted)

1/4 cup chopped fresh parsley

1. Preheat air fryer at 180°C for 3 minutes.
2. In a large bowl, combine potatoes, garlic and melted butter.
3. Place potato mixture in air fryer basket. Cook for 7 minutes. Toss. Cook for an additional 7 minutes. Transfer to a large bowl.
4. Add salt, pepper, half the cream and 1 tablespoon butter and mash. Slowly add remaining cream until desired consistency.
5. Garnish with parsley and serve warm.

PER SERVING

KILOJOULES: 849 | **FAT:** 13.4g | **PROTEIN:** 2.4g | **SODIUM:** 315mg | **FIBRE:** 2.7g | **CARBOHYDRATES:** 17.8g | **SUGAR:** 1.7g

ALTERNATIVES TO THICKENED CREAM

Ahhhh… thickened cream. It's thick and it's creamy! Sometimes we only use this when guests come over and we want to put our best foodie foot forward. But for our everyday consumption, a lower caloric punch is welcomed. Use light thickened cream or full-cream milk. Or, if you are a vegan or dairy upsets your gut health, unsweetened almond milk can work just as well!

Curly Fries

To obtain these cute curly fries, you'll need a spiralizer. The spiralizer will cut the entire potato into curls; once completed, cut the curls in 8cm lengths to obtain "fries".

- **Hands-On Time:** 10 minutes
- **Cook Time:** 13 minutes

Serves 2

2 medium potatoes, scrubbed and spiraled into curls, then cut into 8cm lengths (see above)
3 teaspoons salt, divided
2 teaspoons olive oil
¼ teaspoon freshly ground black pepper

1. Place fries in a medium saucepan. Cover fries with water. Add 1 teaspoon salt. Bring to a boil. Boil for 2–3 minutes. Drain.
2. Preheat air fryer at 200°C for 3 minutes.
3. Toss fries with olive oil and 1 teaspoon salt. Place fries in fryer basket and cook for 4 minutes. Shake basket. Cook for an additional 4 minutes. Shake. Season with pepper and remaining teaspoon salt. Cook for an additional 5 minutes.
4. Transfer fries to a plate and serve warm.

PER SERVING (1 CUP)

KILOJOULES: 610 | **FAT:** 4.5g | **PROTEIN:** 2.3g | **SODIUM:** 2,618mg | **FIBRE:** 2.5g | **CARBOHYDRATES:** 24.8g | **SUGAR:** 1.1g

Crispy French Fries

By boiling the potatoes prior to air frying, the centre becomes tender and the exterior gets that nice crunch from the air fryer. There's no need for going out to satisfy that French fry craving when this healthier alternative is so easy to achieve.

- **Hands-On Time:** `10 minutes
- **Cook Time:** 18 minutes

Serves 4

2 medium potatoes, scrubbed and cut lengthwise into 6mm fries
3 teaspoons salt, divided
2 teaspoons olive oil

1. Place fries in a medium saucepan. Cover fries with water. Add 1 teaspoon salt. Bring to a boil. Boil for 3 minutes until fork-tender. Drain.
2. Preheat air fryer at 200°C for 3 minutes.
3. In a medium bowl, toss fries with olive oil and 1 teaspoon salt. Place fries in fryer basket and cook for 5 minutes. Shake basket. Cook for an additional 5 minutes. Shake. Season with remaining teaspoon salt. Cook for an additional 5 minutes.
4. Transfer fries to a plate and serve warm.

PER SERVING

KILOJOULES: 326 | **FAT:** 2.2g | **PROTEIN:** 1.3g | **SODIUM:** 1,325mg | **FIBRE:** 1.4g | **CARBOHYDRATES:** 13.7g | **SUGAR:** .6g

Savoury Sweet Potato Fries

The savoury spices of onion powder and smoked paprika play well with the natural sugars in the sweet potato. Both crisp and tender, these fries are a healthy snack option or tasty side for a juicy burger!

- **Hands-On Time:** 10 minutes
- **Cook Time:** 15 minutes

Serves 2

1 large sweet potato, peeled and cut lengthwise into 6mm fries
¾ tablespoon olive oil
¼ teaspoon salt
¼ teaspoon onion powder
¼ teaspoon smoked paprika

1. Preheat air fryer at 190°C for 3 minutes.
2. In a medium bowl, toss fries with olive oil, salt, onion powder and paprika. Place fries in fryer basket and cook for 5 minutes. Shake basket. Cook for an additional 5 minutes. Shake. Cook for an additional 5 minutes.
3. Transfer to a serving bowl. Serve warm.

PER SERVING

KILOJOULES: 485 | **FAT:** 6.6g | **PROTEIN:** 1.1g | **SODIUM:** 326mg | **FIBRE:** 2.1g | **CARBOHYDRATES:** 13.5g | **SUGAR:** 2.8g

Butternut Pumpkin Fries

If you can't find butternut pumpkin fries precut, simply use a vegetable peeler to remove the skin, slice squash lengthwise and use a spoon to scrape out and discard the seeds, then cut flesh into 6mm fries.

- **Hands-On Time:** 10 minutes
- **Cook Time:** 15 minutes

Serves 2

570 grams butternut pumpkin fries, pre-cut or home-cut, or about 1 large pumpkin
¾ tablespoon olive oil
½ teaspoon cinnamon
½ teaspoon ground ginger
Pinch cayenne pepper
½ teaspoon salt

1. Preheat air fryer at 190°C for 3 minutes.
2. In a medium bowl, toss fries with olive oil, cinnamon, ground ginger, cayenne pepper and salt. Place fries in fryer basket and cook for 5 minutes. Shake basket. Cook for an additional 5 minutes. Shake. Cook for an additional 5 minutes.
3. Transfer to a serving bowl and serve warm.

PER SERVING

KILOJOULES: 794 | **FAT:** 6.8g | **PROTEIN:** 2.9g | **SODIUM:** 592mg | **FIBRE:** 6.1g | **CARBOHYDRATES:** 34.0g | **SUGAR:** 6.3g

Baby Bacon Hasselbacks

If a baked potato and home fries had a baby, it'd be this dish. The slices of potatoes allow the melted butter to cook down in the nooks and crannies, creating multiple crisp edges, and the bacon between slices makes a salty pork flavour that only bacon can give.

- **Hands-On Time:** 15 minutes
- **Cook Time:** 20 minutes

Serves 3

6 baby red potatoes, scrubbed
1 slice uncooked bacon, diced
3/4 tablespoon olive oil
1 1/2 tablespoons butter, melted
Pinch salt
6 teaspoons sour cream
1/4 cup chopped fresh parsley

1. Make slices in the width of potatoes about 6mm apart without cutting all the way through. Press a small dice of bacon between each slice. Brush potatoes with olive oil.
2. Preheat air fryer at 180°C for 3 minutes.
3. Add potatoes to air fryer basket. Cook for 10 minutes. Brush with melted butter, ensuring the butter gets between slices. Cook for an additional 10 minutes.
4. Transfer potatoes to a serving dish. Season with salt. Add a dollop of sour cream to the top of each potato. Garnish with chopped parsley. Serve warm.

PER SERVING

KILOJOULES: 1602 | **FAT:** 14.8g | **PROTEIN:** 8.2g | **SODIUM:** 181mg | **FIBRE:** 6.0g | **CARBOHYDRATES:** 54.7g | **SUGAR:** 4.7g

Baked Gnocchi

Gnocchi are pillowy little potato dumplings that are traditionally served with a rich sauce. In this recipe, the pillows are still fluffy, but the air fryer gives them a crispy exterior.

- **Hands-On Time:** 5 minutes
- **Cook Time:** 27 minutes

Serves 4

2 medium potatoes, peeled and diced
½ teaspoon onion powder
½ teaspoon salt
½ teaspoon freshly ground black pepper
1 large egg
¼ cup plain flour
¾ tablespoon butter, melted
½ teaspoon garlic salt

1. Add potatoes to a large pot with enough water to cover potatoes. Bring to boil. Reduce heat and simmer for 4–5 minutes until potatoes are fork-tender.
2. Drain potatoes and transfer to a medium bowl. Add onion powder, salt and pepper to the bowl. Mash seasoned potatoes until smooth. Add egg and mix until combined.
3. Sprinkle some of the flour on a flat, clean surface. With floured hands, knead dough to incorporate some of the flour and reduce stickiness.
4. Break off a small ball of dough. Work into a rope 1cm wide. Using a knife cut into 1cm sections. If you'd like the classic lines on the gnocchi, roll each gnocchi under the tines of a fork. Repeat with the rest of the dough.
5. Bring a pot of salted water to a boil. Add gnocchi in two batches to water. Using a slotted spoon, remove once they rise to the top, after about 2 minutes.
6. Preheat air fryer at 180°C for 3 minutes.
7. Add gnocchi to air fryer basket. Cook for 5 minutes. Gently toss. Cook for another 5 minutes. Toss and brush gnocchi with butter. Cook for 4 minutes. Toss again and cook for an additional 4 minutes.
8. Transfer gnocchi to a bowl and toss with garlic salt. Serve warm.

PER SERVING

KILOJOULES: 485 | **FAT:** 3.8g | **PROTEIN:** 3.1g | **SODIUM:** 754mg | **FIBRE:** 1.8g | **CARBOHYDRATES:** 17.2g | **SUGAR:** 0.8g

Cajun-Fried Sweet Pickle Chips

This is a sweet and spicy twist on the classic dill pickle version. Read the seasoning labels on your Cajun seasoning, as some can deliver quite a punch in the heat department.

- **Hands-On Time:** 10 minutes
- **Cook Time:** 16 minutes

Serves 4

450 grams jar sweet pickles, drained, cut in rounds
2 large eggs
¼ cup full-cream milk
½ cup plain bread crumbs
¼ cup polenta
¼ teaspoon salt
1 ½ tablespoons Cajun seasoning

1. Pat pickles dry between paper towels.
2. In a small bowl, whisk together eggs and milk.
3. Combine bread crumbs, polenta, salt and Cajun seasoning in a shallow dish.
4. Preheat air fryer at 200° for 3 minutes.
5. Dip pickle slices in egg mixture. Coat in polenta mixture, shaking off any excess.
6. Add half of pickle slices to fryer basket and cook for 4 minutes. Shake and flip pickles. Cook for an additional 4 minutes.
7. Transfer to a plate. Repeat with remaining pickles.

PER SERVING

KILOJOULES: 2502 | **FAT:** 2.8g | **PROTEIN:** 5.7g | **SODIUM:** 2,119mg | **FIBRE:** 1.9g | **CARBOHYDRATES:** 22.9g | **SUGAR:** 2.4g

Fried Green Beans

These green beans are quick and crispy and perfect for snacking on while enjoying a cold brew. Also, if you have some picky eaters, these may be the trick to get them to try something green!

- **Hands-On Time:** 10 minutes
- **Cook Time:** 14 minutes

Serves 2

1 large egg
3/4 tablespoon full-cream milk
3/4 tablespoon honey
1 1/2 tablespoons polenta
1 1/2 tablespoons cornflour
1 1/2 tablespoons finely grated Parmesan cheese
1/2 teaspoon salt, plus an extra pinch for garnish
230 grams green beans, trimmed (about 3 cups)

HOW DO YOU "TRIM" GREEN BEANS?

You may say "trimming" green beans, but a cooking term that means the same thing is to "top and tail" the beans. If the beans are young and fresh, you only need to line up a handful of the stem end of the beans and give one uniform chop, then repeat with the remaining beans. However, if the beans are more mature, after you slice off the stem ends you'll have to cut the opposite end off one at a time and then gently pull the string off and discard it.

1. In a medium bowl, whisk together egg, milk and honey.
2. In a shallow dish, combine polenta, cornflour, cheese and salt.
3. Preheat air fryer at 190°C for 3 minutes.
4. Coat green beans with egg mixture and shake off any excess. Coat in the polenta mixture.
5. Place green beans in air fryer basket. Cook for 7 minutes. Gently toss green beans. Cook for an additional 7 minutes.
6. Transfer green beans to a serving dish and garnish with a pinch of salt. Serve warm.

PER SERVING

KILOJOULES: 715 | **FAT:** 2.9g | **PROTEIN:** 6.7g | **SODIUM:** 774mg | **FIBRE:** 4.5g | **CARBOHYDRATES:** 31.0g | **SUGAR:** 9.8g

Asian Brussels Sprouts

The saltiness of the soy sauce and the sweetness of the maple syrup help counter the bitter flavour that some may detect in Brussels sprouts. Rounded out even more with the small kick of heat from the sriracha, this side dish will have your family asking for seconds!

- **Hands-On Time:** 5 minutes
- **Cook Time:** 14 minutes

Serves 2

1/4 cup freshly squeezed orange juice
3/4 tablespoon pure maple syrup
3/4 tablespoon soy sauce
1/4 teaspoon sriracha
3/4 tablespoon olive oil
450 grams Brussels sprouts, halved
Pinch salt

1 In a large bowl, whisk together orange juice, maple syrup, soy sauce, sriracha and olive oil. Toss in Brussels sprouts. Refrigerate 30 minutes.

2 Preheat air fryer at 180°C for 3 minutes.

3 Add Brussels sprouts to air fryer. Cook for 7 minutes. Toss. Cook for an additional 7 minutes.

4 Transfer Brussels sprouts to a serving dish, season with salt and serve warm.

PER SERVING

KILOJOULES: 524 | **FAT:** 3.7g | **PROTEIN:** 6.1g | **SODIUM:** 304mg | **FIBRE:** 6.4g | **CARBOHYDRATES:** 20.2g | **SUGAR:** 8.1g

BRUSSELS SPROUTS: LOVE 'EM OR HATE 'EM?

There are a couple of reasons why some people love Brussels sprouts and others run quickly in the opposite direction. For one, we eat first with our sense of smell, and the Brussels sprout, a cruciferous vegetable, has a bitterness that turns some away immediately. Also, some people are born with more sensitive bitter receptors on the tongue, so their reaction is going to be different from that of someone with less sensitive bitter receptors. Adding flavouring to this vegetable, instead of a simple salt-and-pepper steam job, might convert a few people.

Prosciutto-Wrapped Asparagus

The air fryer knows how to crisp up prosciutto, and wrapped asparagus is a such a bonus. There is no need for seasoning. The salty nature of prosciutto lends just enough flavour for these tasty spears. Enjoy as a side dish, snack or appetiser, either alone or with a homemade dipping sauce!

- **Hands-On Time:** 5 minutes
- **Cook Time:** 12 minutes

Serves 4

85 grams prosciutto
18 thick spears asparagus, trimmed of woody ends

WHY IS SOME ASPARAGUS WHITE?

White asparagus is given special care prior to harvesting so sunlight does not touch it. The plants are grown below mounds of dirt and the result is tender white stalks of asparagus. If you are a true fan, visit Schwetzingen, Germany, which is the *spargel*, or asparagus, capital of the world!

1. Slice prosciutto lengthwise into 18 even slices. Spiral wrap the prosciutto strips from the bottom of the asparagus to the top, stopping before covering the tip.
2. Preheat air fryer at 200°C for 3 minutes.
3. Place wrapped asparagus in air fryer basket. Cook for 6 minutes. Shake. Cook for an additional 6 minutes until prosciutto is crisp.
4. Transfer to a plate and serve.

PER SERVING

KILOJOULES: 334 | **FAT:** 4.8g | **PROTEIN:** 6.5g | **SODIUM:** 86mg | **FIBRE:** 1.9g | **CARBOHYDRATES:** 4.0g | **SUGAR:** 1.7g

Home Fries

These cubed, crispy home fries are accented with browned onions and simply dressed with olive oil, salt, pepper and fresh parsley.

- **Hands-On Time:** 10 minutes
- **Cook Time:** 21 minutes

Serves 2

2 medium potatoes, scrubbed and cut into 3cm cubes
4 teaspoons salt, divided
3 teaspoons olive oil, divided
¼ teaspoon freshly ground black pepper
1 small brown onion, peeled and thinly sliced into half moons
¼ cup chopped fresh parsley

WHAT DOES IT MEAN TO CARAMELISE ONIONS?

Onions contain natural sugars that when heated start to brown or caramelise. But there is a point of contention among chefs when recipes ask you to "caramelise" the onions for 5–10 minutes. Yes, the onions are starting to caramelise, but stopping at this cooking point is called "blonding" the onions. To be considered true caramelisation, the procedure takes 30–40 minutes. And there is an art. They have to be cared for; not crowded in the frying pan, not heated too quickly, and given a deglazing or two with some water, broth, wine or even whiskey during the process!

1. Place potato cubes in a medium saucepan and cover with water. Add 1 teaspoon salt. Bring to a boil and boil for 2–3 minutes. Drain.
2. Preheat air fryer at 200°C for 3 minutes.
3. Place potato cubes in a medium bowl and toss with 2 teaspoons olive oil and 1 teaspoon salt. Place potatoes in fryer basket and cook for 4 minutes. Shake basket. Cook for an additional 4 minutes. Shake. Season with pepper and 1 teaspoon salt. Cook for an additional 4 minutes.
4. Transfer potatoes to a plate and keep warm.
5. While fries are cooking, place onions, 1 teaspoon olive oil and 1 teaspoon salt in a medium frying pan over medium heat. Cook for 5–6 minutes until onions are tender and starting to brown.
6. Combine cooked potatoes and onions in a medium serving dish. Garnish with chopped parsley. Serve warm.

PER SERVING

KILOJOULES: 811 | **FAT:** 6.7g | **PROTEIN:** 3.2g | **SODIUM:** 2,656mg | **FIBRE:** 3.6g | **CARBOHYDRATES:** 31.3g | **SUGAR:** 2.7g

Chilli-Lime Corn Chips

When you're craving chips and salsa, giving in doesn't have to be a diet killer. Make your own chips using corn tortillas. They are seasoned and crispy and *not* deep-fried. Try these with Pico Guacamole (see page 68).

- **Hands-On Time:** 10 minutes
- **Cook Time:** 15 minutes

Serves 4

3/4 tablespoon olive oil
3/4 tablespoon fresh lime juice
6 (15cm) corn tortillas, each cut into 6 triangles
1/2 teaspoon chilli powder
1/2 teaspoon salt

1. Preheat air fryer at 200°C for 3 minutes.
2. In a small bowl, whisk together olive oil and lime juice. Brush over tortilla triangles. Toss with chilli powder.
3. Place a third of the triangles in the air fryer basket. Cook for 3 minutes. Flip and season with salt. Cook for an additional 2 minutes, then transfer to a serving bowl. Repeat with remaining two batches.
4. Let chips cool for 5 minutes before serving.

PER SERVING

KILOJOULES: 456 | **FAT:** 4.3g | **PROTEIN:** 2.1g | **SODIUM:** 316mg | **FIBRE:** 2.4g | **CARBOHYDRATES:** 16.6g | **SUGAR:** 0.4g

Parmesan Potato Chips

Slicing the potato paper-thin and consistently is the key to perfect potato chips. The air fryer will brown the edges, but keep checking them toward the end of the cooking time. They can go from brown to burned quickly!

- **Hands-On Time:** 10 minutes
- **Cook Time:** 17 minutes

Serves 2

1 medium potato, scrubbed and sliced into 3mm-thick circles
2 teaspoons olive oil
1 teaspoon salt, divided
4 teaspoons grated Parmesan cheese, divided

1. In a small bowl, toss potato circles with olive oil and ½ teaspoon salt.
2. Preheat air fryer at 200°C for 3 minutes.
3. Place chips in fryer basket and cook for 6 minutes. Shake basket. Cook for an additional 5 minutes. Shake. Add 2 teaspoons Parmesan cheese and cook for 6 minutes.
4. Transfer to a serving bowl and garnish with remaining salt and Parmesan cheese. Let rest 15 minutes before serving.

PER SERVING

KILOJOULES: 485 | **FAT:** 5.4g | **PROTEIN:** 2.5g | **SODIUM:** 1,400mg | **FIBRE:** 1.4g | **CARBOHYDRATES:** 14.5g | **SUGAR:** 0.6g

Sesame Tortilla Chips

When you want some Asian flair added to your tortilla chips, a little sesame oil and seeds can help achieve this. The addition of the honey sweetens these just enough but does not overpower.

- **Hands-On Time:** 10 minutes
- **Cook Time:** 18 minutes

Serves 4

2 teaspoons sesame oil
2 teaspoons honey
6 (15cm) flour tortillas, each cut into 6 triangles
2 teaspoons sesame seeds
1 teaspoon poppy seeds
½ teaspoon salt

1. Preheat air fryer at 200°C for 3 minutes.
2. In a small bowl, whisk together sesame oil and honey. Brush oil mixture over tortilla triangles. Toss with sesame seeds and poppy seeds.
3. Place a third of the chips in the air fryer basket. Cook for 3 minutes. Flip chips. Cook for an additional 3 minutes. Repeat with remaining two batches.
4. Season chips with salt as they come out of the fryer basket. Let cool for 5 minutes before serving.

PER SERVING

KILOJOULES: 698 | **FAT:** 5.0g | **PROTEIN:** 3.8g | **SODIUM:** 610mg **FIBRE:** 1.3g | **CARBOHYDRATES:** 26.6g | **SUGAR:** 4.4g

Carrot Chips

Although you can use whatever cooking oil you prefer, with these carrot chips, the coconut oil provides a great flavour accent for the carrots.

- **Hands-On Time:** 10 minutes
- **Cook Time:** 12 minutes

Serves 4

2 large carrots, peeled and sliced into paper-thin circles
2 teaspoons coconut oil, melted
¼ teaspoon ground cumin
¼ teaspoon smoked paprika
¼ teaspoon salt
⅛ teaspoon freshly ground black pepper

1. In a medium bowl, toss carrots in coconut oil. Season with cumin, paprika, salt and pepper.
2. Preheat air fryer at 200°C for 3 minutes.
3. Place chips in fryer basket and cook for 12 minutes, shaking every 3 minutes.
4. Transfer to a bowl. Let rest for 10 minutes before serving.

PER SERVING

KILOJOULES: 142 | **FAT:** 2.2g | **PROTEIN:** 0.4g | **SODIUM:** 170mg | **FIBRE:** 1.1g | **CARBOHYDRATES:** 3.7g | **SUGAR:** 1.7g

Sesame Parsnip Chips

Parsnips are the white carrot-looking produce you have probably passed by in the store a million times. They are related to the carrot but have a sweeter and a bit of a peppery flavour. Parsnips are often used as potato replacements in soups and stews.

- **Hands-On Time:** 10 minutes
- **Cook Time:** 14 minutes

Serves 2

1 large parsnip, peeled and sliced into 3mm-thick circles
¾ tablespoon sesame oil
½ teaspoon salt, divided

1. In a small bowl, toss parsnip slices with sesame oil and ¼ teaspoon salt.
2. Preheat air fryer at 200°C for 3 minutes.
3. Place parsnips in fryer basket and cook for 5 minutes. Shake basket. Cook for an additional 5 minutes. Shake. Cook for an additional 4 minutes.
4. Transfer to a serving bowl and garnish with remaining salt. Serve when ready.

PER SERVING

KILOJOULES: 405 | **FAT:** 6.6g | **PROTEIN:** 0.6g | **SODIUM:** 585mg | **FIBRE:** 2.4g | **CARBOHYDRATES:** 9.0g | **SUGAR:** 2.4g

Herbed Zucchini Fries

These breaded, crispy zucchini fries are crave-worthy and will have you buying a bagful of zucchini just so you can keep making them. A healthy alternative to the drive-through French fries, this treat is delicious!

- **Hands-On Time:** 10 minutes
- **Cook Time:** 20 minutes

Serves 2

1 large zucchini, cut in half crosswise, then lengthwise into 6mm fries
1 teaspoon salt
1/2 cup buttermilk
3/4 cup plain bread crumbs
3/4 tablespoon Italian seasoning

1 Scatter zucchini pieces evenly over a paper towel. Sprinkle with salt. Let zucchini sit for 10 minutes to pull out the moisture. Pat with paper towels.

2 Preheat air fryer at 190°C for 3 minutes.

3 Place buttermilk in a shallow dish. Combine bread crumbs and Italian seasoning in a separate shallow dish.

4 Dip zucchini in buttermilk. Coat in bread crumb mixture.

5 Place half of zucchini pieces in fryer basket and cook for 5 minutes. Flip fries. Cook for an additional 5 minutes.

6 Transfer to a serving dish. Repeat with remaining zucchini fries and serve warm.

PER SERVING

KILOJOULES: 723 | **FAT:** 2.5g | **PROTEIN:** 8.0g | **SODIUM:** 1,156mg | **FIBRE:** 3.0g | **CARBOHYDRATES:** 29.4g | **SUGAR:** 8.5g

Sweet Chilli Baby Bok Choy

Air frying these baby clusters of bok choy makes tender cabbage with crispy edges. The homemade sweet chilli sauce balances out the slight bitterness of the bok choy. Serve alongside a piece of cod for a light and healthy meal.

- **Hands-On Time:** 10 minutes
- **Cook Time:** 12 minutes

Serves 4

2 medium clusters baby bok choy, quartered lengthwise
¹⁄₄ cup Sweet Chilli Sauce (see page 73)
Pinch salt

WHAT IS BOK CHOY?

Native to China, bok choy is most closely related to cabbage. Traditionally found in stir-fries and kimchi (Korean fermented veggies), bok choy is also a crunchy alternative in coleslaw and is beautiful brushed with oil and grilled next to your steak. High in vitamins and nutrients, this vegetable is a powerhouse that will be welcomed by all in the family!

1. Clean quartered baby bok choy and let drain on paper towels. Pat dry.
2. Preheat air fryer at 180°C for 3 minutes.
3. Brush bok choy with sweet chilli sauce. Place half in air fryer basket and cook for 3 minutes. Flip bok choy. Cook for an additional 3 minutes. Repeat with remaining bok choy.
4. Transfer to a serving plate, season with a pinch of salt and serve warm.

PER SERVING

KILOJOULES: 560 | **FAT:** 0.3g | **PROTEIN:** 3.3g | **SODIUM:** 255mg | **FIBRE:** 2.1g | **CARBOHYDRATES:** 31.0g | **SUGAR:** 27.7g

Fried Corn on the Cob

There's nothing better than sweet, juicy corn. Not only will the air fryer cook the corn cobs in half the time, but the addition of Parmesan cheese will create a crispy, cheesy exterior.

- **Hands-On Time:** 5 minutes
- **Cook Time:** 20 minutes

Serves 4

1 large egg
1 cup buttermilk
1 cup plain flour
2 teaspoons salt
1/2 teaspoon sugar
1 teaspoon dried thyme
1/4 cup grated Parmesan cheese
4 corn cobs, shucked and halved, silk removed
2 1/4 tablespoons butter, melted

BUTTERMILK SUBSTITUTES

If you don't have buttermilk on hand, simply mix together 1 cup full-cream milk and 1 tablespoon lemon juice. Let stand for 5 minutes. This will give enough time to allow the milk to curdle. Another option is to whisk together 1/4 cup full-cream milk and 3/4 cup plain yoghurt.

1. In a medium bowl, whisk together egg and buttermilk.
2. In a shallow dish, combine flour, salt, sugar, thyme and Parmesan cheese.
3. Preheat air fryer at 200°C for 3 minutes.
4. Roll corn in egg mixture and coat in flour mixture. Shake off excess.
5. Add 4 half corn cobs to fryer basket and cook for 7 minutes. Flip corn and brush with melted butter. Cook for an additional 3 minutes. Repeat with remaining corn.
6. Transfer fried corn to a plate and serve warm.

PER SERVING

KILOJOULES: 1087 | **FAT:** 11.3g | **PROTEIN:** 8.0g | **SODIUM:** 694mg | **FIBRE:** 2.5g | **CARBOHYDRATES:** 33.5g | **SUGAR:** 8.4g

Walnut-Crusted Goat Cheese Bombs

Whether serving these beside a juicy steak, adding a fresh twist to a summer salad or just popping them in your mouth, these walnut-crusted goat cheese bombs will add smiles to the faces of all those around you.

- **Hands-On Time:** 10 minutes
- **Cook Time:** 16 minutes

Serves 4

140 grams goat cheese, at room temperature
140 grams mascarpone cheese, at room temperature
¼ teaspoon salt
¼ teaspoon freshly ground black pepper
1 teaspoon fresh thyme leaves
¼ cup plain flour
1 large egg, whisked
⅓ cup finely crushed walnuts
⅓ cup panko bread crumbs

1. In a medium bowl, combine goat cheese, mascarpone cheese, salt, pepper and thyme. Form into 16 balls of equal size.
2. Add flour to a small bowl. Add whisked egg to another small bowl. Mix walnut crumbs and bread crumbs in a shallow dish.
3. Roll cheese bombs in flour. Shake off any excess. Dip cheese bombs in egg. Shake off any excess. Coat cheese bombs in bread crumb mixture. Place coated cheese bombs in freezer for 30 minutes.
4. Preheat air fryer at 190°C for 3 minutes.
5. Add eight cheese bombs to lightly greased air fryer basket. Cook for 8 minutes. Repeat with remaining cheese bombs.
6. Transfer to a serving plate and serve warm.

PER SERVING

KILOJOULES: 1414 | **FAT:** 24.7g | **PROTEIN:** 13.5g | **SODIUM:** 338mg | **FIBRE:** 0.6g | **CARBOHYDRATES:** 14.0g | **SUGAR:** 1.9g

WHAT IS MASCARPONE CHEESE?

Mascarpone (pronounced mahs-kar-POH-nay) is just an Italian version of cream cheese. Cream cheese is slightly tangier, and mascarpone cheese has a higher fat content, so if splitting hairs, I'm sure some chefs will argue the difference; however, for most home chefs, consider that these unripened cheeses are pretty much interchangeable in recipes.

Blistered Grape Tomatoes

Adding heat to tomatoes brings out their natural sugars. Tossed with tangy balsamic vinegar, this side dish is an excellent accompaniment to a steak fresh off the BBQ.

- **Hands-On Time:** 5 minutes
- **Cook Time:** 15 minutes

Serves 4

225 grams (approximately 30) grape tomatoes
2 teaspoons olive oil
1/4 teaspoon salt
3/4 tablespoon balsamic vinegar
3/4 tablespoon chopped fresh basil

CAN I USE OTHER TOMATO VARIETIES TO BLISTER?

Of course! Grape tomatoes are small, oval tomatoes with a sweet flavour, but there are other varieties of baby tomatoes that benefit from the char flavour. Cherry tomatoes, pear tomatoes (both red and yellow) and Super Sweet 100s are all terrific choices for blistering.

1. Preheat air fryer at 180°C for 3 minutes.
2. In a small bowl, toss tomatoes, olive oil and salt.
3. Transfer tomatoes to air fryer basket and cook for 5 minutes. Shake basket. Cook for 5 minutes. Shake basket. Cook for 5 minutes.
4. Transfer tomatoes to a bowl. Toss with balsamic vinegar and garnish with chopped basil.

PER SERVING

KILOJOULES: 183 | **FAT:** 2.3g | **PROTEIN:** 0.5g | **SODIUM:** 148mg | **FIBRE:** 0.7g | **CARBOHYDRATES:** 2.9g | **SUGAR:** 2.1g

Roasted Corn Salad

By air frying the corn, you add a little char, which in turn adds a lot of flavour. Refrigerate this salad covered overnight to really allow the flavours to marry together for an even better experience.

- **Hands-On Time:** 5 minutes
- **Cook Time:** 7 minutes

Serves 4

3 corn cobs, shucked and halved, silk removed

2 medium Roma tomatoes, seeded and diced

1 cup canned black beans, drained and rinsed

1 medium avocado, peeled, pitted and diced

½ cup chopped fresh coriander

½ cup diced red onion

¼ cup balsamic vinegar

1 ½ tablespoons olive oil

½ teaspoon salt

¼ teaspoon freshly ground black pepper

1. Preheat air fryer at 200°C for 3 minutes.
2. Add corn to fryer basket and cook for 5 minutes. Shake basket. Cook for an additional 2 minutes.
3. Transfer corn to a plate and allow to cool until easy to handle. Cut kernels from cob and add to a medium bowl.
4. Add remaining ingredients, combine and serve.

PER SERVING

KILOJOULES: 1104 | **FAT:** 12.4g | **PROTEIN:** 7.4g | **SODIUM:** 450mg | **FIBRE:** 8.8g | **CARBOHYDRATES:** 33.1g | **SUGAR:** 9.1g

CORIANDER — YUCK?

Back off coriander; half of us hate you. Oh, but half of us love you so much! Why, you ask? Well, some people have a gene that actually makes coriander taste like soap. So when recipes call for coriander, don't just discard the recipe altogether. Depending on the recipe, use your judgment and substitute fresh parsley or mint. It won't taste the same as coriander, but it will add that fresh herb flavour to your dish.

7

Poultry Main Dishes

Prep-Day Chicken Thighs

Chicken thighs are not only easy on the wallet, but are also juicy and delicious. Make these and add them to salads or soups during the week, or just heat them up and eat them as is!

- **Hands-On Time:** 10 minutes
- **Cook Time:** 35 minutes

Serves 4

2 teaspoons olive oil
1.2 kilograms boneless, skinless chicken thighs (approximately 6)
½ teaspoon salt
¼ teaspoon freshly ground black pepper

1. Brush oil lightly over chicken. Season with salt and pepper.
2. Preheat air fryer at 180°C for 3 minutes.
3. Add chicken to fryer basket and cook for 35 minutes.
4. Using a meat thermometer, assure that the chicken is at least 75°C. Transfer to a serving plate and let rest for 5 minutes.
5. Chop and store covered in the refrigerator for some of your week's recipes.

PER SERVING

KILOJOULES: 866 | **FAT:** 9.9g | **PROTEIN:** 26.0g | **SODIUM:** 401mg | **FIBRE:** 0.0g | **CARBOHYDRATES:** 0.1g | **SUGAR:** 0.0g

ARE CHICKEN THIGHS FATTY?

Although chicken thighs (the dark meat) contain more fat than the chicken breast (white meat), both are excellent sources of lean protein. One advantage of chicken thighs is that they are more economical than breasts. Another is that because of the fattier nature of the thighs, they are less likely to dry out than white meat during the cooking process. And as far as flavour? Well, chicken thighs win!

Italian Stuffed Chicken Breasts

The air fryer and breading give this chicken a beautiful coating and ensure that the chicken remains tender.

- **Hands-On Time:** 10 minutes
- **Cook Time:** 18 minutes

Serves 8

1 large egg
1 1/2 cups full-cream milk
1 cup plain bread crumbs
3/4 tablespoon Italian seasoning
2 boneless, skinless chicken breasts (approximately 450 grams)
1/4 teaspoon salt
1/4 teaspoon freshly ground black pepper
1 1/2 tablespoons cream cheese
2 teaspoons Dijon mustard
4 slices jarred roasted red peppers
4 slices deli ham
2 tablespoons butter, melted

1. In a medium bowl, whisk together egg and milk.
2. In a shallow dish, combine bread crumbs and Italian seasoning.
3. Between two pieces of baking paper, pound chicken breasts to 6mm thickness. Season with salt and pepper.
4. Spread a layer of half the cream cheese and then half the mustard on each chicken breast. Add 2 pepper slices and 2 ham slices on each. Roll tightly from short end to short end.
5. Preheat air fryer at 190°C for 3 minutes.
6. Carefully dip chicken rolls in egg mixture. Coat in bread crumbs. Shake off any excess.
7. Add rolled chicken to air fryer basket. Cook for 10 minutes. Brush tops with melted butter. Cook for an additional 8 minutes.
8. Transfer to a cutting board. Let rolled chicken rest for 5 minutes. Slice each breast into four rounds and serve warm.

PER SERVING

KILOJOULES: 1363 | **FAT:** 15.4g | **PROTEIN:** 34.5g | **SODIUM:** 1,147mg | **FIBRE:** 1.5g | **CARBOHYDRATES:** 18.5g | **SUGAR:** 3.1g

Buttermilk Southern-Fried Chicken Legs

These fried chicken legs are crisp on the outside and juicy on the inside. The buttermilk lends a citric quality, adding flavour as well as the ability to tenderise the meat and create a crispier skin.

- **Hands-On Time:** 10 minutes
- **Cook Time:** 36 minutes

Serves 3

2.5 kilograms boneless, skinless chicken legs (approximately 5-6)
1 cup buttermilk
1 cup plain bread crumbs
1 teaspoon smoked paprika
1 teaspoon garlic powder
Pinch ground nutmeg
1 teaspoon salt
1 teaspoon freshly ground black pepper
2 1/4 tablespoons butter, melted

DOES A PINCH OF NUTMEG REALLY MAKE A DIFFERENCE?

Yes, yes, yes! Don't just think about gingerbread when considering using nutmeg. It is so aromatic and unique that just a dash in sauces, casseroles and even soups will make your guests not only gasp in delight but start scratching their head wondering what that spice is.

1. In a medium bowl, place chicken legs and buttermilk and marinate in the refrigerator covered for 30 minutes up to overnight.
2. Preheat air fryer at 180°C for 3 minutes.
3. Combine bread crumbs, paprika, garlic powder, nutmeg, salt and pepper in a shallow dish. Shake excess buttermilk off chicken legs and coat in bread crumb mixture. Set aside.
4. Add half of chicken to lightly greased fryer basket and cook for 10 minutes.
5. Brush lightly with melted butter. Flip chicken. Brush other side lightly with butter. Increase temperature to 200°C. Cook for an additional 8 minutes. Using a meat thermometer, assure that the chicken is at least 75°C.
6. Transfer to a serving plate. Repeat cooking process with remaining chicken and serve warm.

PER SERVING

KILOJOULES: 2765 | **FAT:** 28.3g | **PROTEIN:** 71.2g | **SODIUM:** 904mg | **FIBRE:** 1.2g | **CARBOHYDRATES:** 18.0g | **SUGAR:** 3.8g

Sesame Chicken Legs

The combination of soy sauce, honey, sriracha and lime come together to lend a beautiful balance of Asian flavours. The toasted sesame seed garnish has a little nuttiness and gives another layer of crunch to these crispy chicken legs.

- **Hands-On Time:** 5 minutes
- **Cook Time:** 36 minutes

Serves 6

1/4 cup soy sauce
1/4 cup honey
3/4 tablespoon sriracha
Juice of 1 small lime
2.5 kilograms chicken legs (approximately 5–6)
1 cup plain bread crumbs
1 teaspoon salt
2 1/4 tablespoons butter, melted
1 1/2 tablespoons toasted sesame seeds

HOW TO TOAST SESAME SEEDS

Although sesame seeds are sometimes sold already toasted, if you can only get plain ones, it is easy to toast them on your own. Simply place seeds in a dry frying pan over medium-high heat. Using a wooden spatula, continuously push seeds around the pan 2–4 minutes until golden brown. Immediately transfer to a bowl, as overcooking them will create a bitter flavour.

1. In a medium bowl, combine soy sauce, honey, sriracha and lime juice. Toss chicken legs in sauce. Refrigerate covered for 30 minutes or up to overnight.
2. Preheat air fryer at 180°C for 3 minutes.
3. Combine bread crumbs and salt in a shallow dish. Shake excess sauce off chicken legs and coat in bread crumb mixture. Set aside.
4. Lightly spray or brush fryer basket with oil. Add half of chicken to fryer basket and cook for 10 minutes.
5. Brush lightly with melted butter. Flip chicken. Brush other side lightly with butter. Increase temperature to 200°. Cook for an additional 8 minutes. Using a meat thermometer, assure that the chicken is at least 75°C.
6. Transfer to a serving plate. Repeat cooking process with remaining chicken.
7. Garnish with toasted sesame seeds and serve warm.

PER SERVING

KILOJOULES: 3606 | **FAT:** 36.6g | **PROTEIN:** 92.7g | **SODIUM:** 1,270mg | **FIBRE:** 1.2g | **CARBOHYDRATES:** 23.9g | **SUGAR:** 4.1g

Ritzy Chicken Meatballs

Ground chicken can tend to be a little dry, but with the onions and the buttery nature of the Ritz crackers, these meatballs are juicy and delicious.

- **Hands-On Time:** 10 minutes
- **Cook Time:** 16 minutes

Serves 2

450 grams chicken mince
1 large egg
¾ cup crushed Ritz crackers
¼ cup finely diced brown onion
1 teaspoon Italian seasoning
1 teaspoon salt
½ teaspoon freshly ground black pepper
¼ cup chopped fresh parsley

1. Preheat air fryer at 180°C for 3 minutes.
2. In a medium bowl, combine chicken, egg, crackers, onion, Italian seasoning, salt and pepper. Form into 18 meatballs, about 2 tablespoons each.
3. Add half of meatballs to fryer basket and cook for 6 minutes. Flip meatballs. Cook for an additional 2 minutes. Transfer to serving dish.
4. Repeat with remaining meatballs and garnish with chopped parsley.

PER SERVING

KILOJOULES: 1891 | **FAT:** 22.4g | **PROTEIN:** 37.4g | **SODIUM:** 1,572mg | **FIBRE:** 1.4g | **CARBOHYDRATES:** 21.8g | **SUGAR:** 3.4g

Mexican Chicken Burgers

Flavoured with cumin and chilli powder, these burgers get their moisture from the red onion and diced green chillies. They're great served alone, or you can melt queso fresco atop the patties, add a slice of tomato and some Sriracha Mayonnaise (see page 72), and eat on a bun.

- **Hands-On Time:** 10 minutes
- **Cook Time:** 26 minutes

Serves 2

450 grams chicken mince
1½ tablespoons minced red onion
1 large egg white
¼ cup panko bread crumbs
½ tablespoons canned diced green chillies
1 tablespoon chilli powder
½ teaspoon ground cumin
Pinch salt

1. Preheat air fryer at 180°C for 3 minutes.
2. In a medium bowl, combine all the ingredients and form into four patties, making a slight indentation in the middle of each burger.
3. Add two patties to lightly greased fryer basket and cook for 6 minutes. Flip burgers and cook for an additional 7 minutes or until cooked to your liking. Repeat with remaining burgers.
4. Transfer to a serving plate and serve warm.

PER SERVING

KILOJOULES: 866 | **FAT:** 9.3g | **PROTEIN:** 22.1g | **SODIUM:** 216mg | **FIBRE:** 1.2g | **CARBOHYDRATES:** 7.9g | **SUGAR:** 1.0g

Sage Turkey Legs

Big turkey legs are just fun. Serve with corn on the cob and a chunk of crunchy bread or anything else that can be picked up with your hands. The rubbed sage adds a piney element that conjures up memories of the holidays.

- **Hands-On Time:** 10 minutes
- **Cook Time:** 26 minutes

Serves 2

- **1 1/2 tablespoons Dijon mustard**
- **1 1/2 tablespoons olive oil**
- **3/4 tablespoon apple cider vinegar**
- **1/2 teaspoon rubbed sage**
- **1/2 teaspoon salt**
- **1/4 teaspoon freshly ground black pepper**
- **2 medium turkey legs (about 680 grams total)**

1. In a large plastic resealable bag, combine mustard, oil, vinegar, sage, salt and pepper. Add turkey legs. Seal and massage mixture into legs. Refrigerate for 30 minutes or up to overnight.
2. Preheat air fryer at 180°C for 3 minutes.
3. Place turkey legs in air fryer basket. Cook for 8 minutes. Turn legs a third. Cook for 9 minutes. Turn legs another third. Cook for 9 more minutes. Using a meat thermometer, ensure that the internal temperature is at least 75°C.
4. Transfer to a plate and let rest for 5 minutes. Serve warm.

PER SERVING

KILOJOULES: 5384 | **FAT:** 61.9g | **PROTEIN:** 153.4g | **SODIUM:** 792mg | **FIBRE:** 0.1g | **CARBOHYDRATES:** 1.6g | **SUGAR:** 0.0g

Chicken, Mushrooms and Potatoes

This dish is proof that a full-bodied, tasty meal doesn't have to break the bank. This is also a good recipe to make on a prep day and divide into individual containers for ready-made lunches.

- **Hands-On Time:** 10 minutes
- **Cook Time:** 20 minutes

Serves 2

2 chicken thighs (about 230 grams)
½ teaspoon salt
½ teaspoon freshly ground black pepper
110 grams white mushrooms, quartered
110 grams fingerling potatoes, scrubbed and thinly sliced
2 teaspoons cooking sherry
410 grams canned fire-roasted diced tomatoes, including juice

1. Preheat air fryer at 180°C for 3 minutes.
2. Place chicken thighs in a round cake barrel (accessory). Season with salt and pepper. Add mushrooms and potatoes. Pour sherry and diced tomatoes including juice over chicken, mushrooms and potatoes.
3. Cook for 20 minutes. Using a meat thermometer, ensure that the internal temperature is at least 75°C.
4. Remove barrel from air fryer and let rest for 10 minutes. Serve warm.

PER SERVING

KILOJOULES: 1209 | **FAT:** 10.6g | **PROTEIN:** 22.9g | **SODIUM:** 1,073mg | **FIBRE:** 4.8g | **CARBOHYDRATES:** 22.6g | **SUGAR:** 6.5g

Honey Mustard Chicken Bites

Marinating these chicken bites in the honey mustard and then using some of the unused sauce for dipping doubles up on the sweet and savoury flavour combination.

- **Hands-On Time:** 10 minutes
- **Cook Time:** 18 minutes

Serves 2

1 large egg
1 1/2 tablespoons honey
1 1/2 tablespoons Dijon mustard
1 teaspoon apple cider vinegar
2 boneless, skinless chicken breasts (approximately 450 grams), cut into 3cm cubes
1 cup plain bread crumbs
1 teaspoon salt
1 teaspoon freshly ground black pepper

1. In a medium bowl, whisk together egg, honey, mustard and vinegar. Toss in chicken cubes. Refrigerate covered for 30 minutes or up to overnight.
2. Preheat air fryer at 180°C for 3 minutes.
3. In a shallow dish, combine bread crumbs, salt and pepper. Shake excess marinade off each piece of chicken and then coat in bread crumb mixture.
4. Add chicken cubes in two batches to air fryer basket. Cook for 4 minutes. Shake gently. Cook for an additional 5 minutes. Check the chicken using a meat thermometer to ensure the internal temperature is at least 75°C.
5. Transfer chicken to a serving plate and serve warm.

PER SERVING

KILOJOULES: 1727 | **FAT:** 8.6g | **PROTEIN:** 54.0g | **SODIUM:** 1,333mg | **FIBRE:** 1.4g | **CARBOHYDRATES:** 29.2g | **SUGAR:** 10.4g

Sesame-Orange Chicken

This sesame-orange chicken is healthy, time-saving and affordable. To cut down on cost even more, you can use chicken thighs. They are equally as wonderful.

- **Hands-On Time:** 10 minutes
- **Cook Time:** 18 minutes

Serves 4

1/3 cup freshly squeezed orange juice
1 1/2 tablespoons sesame oil
1/4 cup honey
1 1/2 tablespoons soy sauce
1 teaspoon peeled and minced fresh ginger
1 teaspoon sriracha
2 boneless, skinless chicken breasts (approximately 450 grams), cut into 3cm cubes
1 1/2 cups plain bread crumbs
1 teaspoon salt
4 cups cooked rice
1/4 cup chopped fresh coriander

THE EASY WAY TO PEEL GINGER

Fresh ginger can seem difficult to navigate, with its uneven surface and all the branches. Instead of taking your fingers' safety into the war zone, simply use the edge of a spoon to scrape the peel off of a fresh piece of ginger root before you grate or mince it.

1. In a medium bowl, whisk together orange juice, oil, honey, soy sauce, ginger and sriracha. Pour half of mixture into a small bowl and set aside.
2. Toss chicken cubes in the medium bowl with sauce mixture and refrigerate covered for 30 minutes.
3. In a shallow dish, combine bread crumbs and salt. Shake excess marinade off each piece of chicken and then dredge in bread crumb mixture.
4. Preheat air fryer at 180°C for 3 minutes.
5. Add chicken bites in two batches to air fryer basket. Cook for 4 minutes. Shake gently and flip chicken. Cook for an additional 5 minutes. Check the chicken using a meat thermometer to ensure the internal temperature is at least 75°C.
6. Transfer to a serving plate and drizzle with remaining marinade.
7. Serve chicken warm over rice and garnish with coriander.

PER SERVING

KILOJOULES: 1945 | **FAT:** 7.3g | **PROTEIN:** 30.7g | **SODIUM:** 821mg | **FIBRE:** 1.4g | **CARBOHYDRATES:** 68.4g | **SUGAR:** 14.5g

Chicken Salad with Strawberries and Pecans

Whether you serve this on bread, in lettuce wraps or straight off the spoon, the strawberries add such a fresh twist on this classic salad. The crunch from the pecans gives a textural element that adds another welcome surprise!

- **Hands-On Time:** 10 minutes
- **Cook Time:** 18 minutes

Serves 4

2 boneless, skinless chicken breasts (approximately 450 grams), cut into 3cm cubes
1 teaspoon salt
1/4 teaspoon freshly ground black pepper
3/4 cup mayonnaise
3/4 tablespoon fresh lime juice
1/2 cup chopped pecans
1/2 cup finely chopped celery
1/2 cup diced strawberries

1. Preheat air fryer at 180°C for 3 minutes.
2. Season chicken with salt and pepper.
3. Add chicken cubes in two batches to air fryer basket. Cook for 4 minutes. Shake gently and flip chicken. Cook for an additional 5 minutes. Check the chicken using a meat thermometer to ensure the internal temperature is at least 75°C.
4. Transfer to a plate and cool.
5. Chop chicken and add to a medium bowl. Add remaining ingredients and combine well. Refrigerate covered until ready to eat.

PER SERVING

KILOJOULES: 2108 | **FAT:** 42.4g | **PROTEIN:** 26.0g | **SODIUM:** 1,028mg | **FIBRE:** 1.9g | **CARBOHYDRATES:** 4.4g | **SUGAR:** 1.9g

Asian Turkey Burgers

The sweetness of the orange marmalade is a natural complement to the Asian seasonings in these turkey burgers. You can serve them as is or on a bun with your favourite toppings.

- **Hands-On Time:** 10 minutes
- **Cook Time:** 26 minutes

Serves 4

450 grams turkey mince
1 spring onion, trimmed and finely diced
1 large egg white
1/4 cup panko bread crumbs
3/4 tablespoon orange marmalade
2 teaspoons sriracha
1 teaspoon soy sauce
1 teaspoon ground ginger
Pinch salt

1. Preheat air fryer at 180°C for 3 minutes.
2. In a medium bowl, combine all the ingredients and form four patties, making a slight indentation in the middle of each patty.
3. Add two patties to lightly greased fryer basket and cook for 6 minutes. Flip burgers and cook for an additional 7 minutes. Repeat with remaining burgers.
4. Transfer to a serving plate and serve warm.

PER SERVING

KILOJOULES: 970 | **FAT:** 9.4g | **PROTEIN:** 25.5g | **SODIUM:** 267mg | **FIBRE:** 0.1g | **CARBOHYDRATES:** 9.4g | **SUGAR:** 3.9g

Spicy Pretzel Chicken Nuggets

There's no need to add salt to this treat; the crushed pretzels lend a saltiness and a distinct flavour separate from plain bread crumbs. If you don't want the heat, skip the sriracha.

- **Hands-On Time:** 10 minutes
- **Cook Time:** 18 minutes

Serves 4

1 large egg
$^{3}/_{4}$ tablespoon sriracha
$^{3}/_{4}$ tablespoon yellow mustard
$^{3}/_{4}$ tablespoon mayonnaise
2 boneless, skinless chicken breasts (approximately 450 grams), cut into 3cm cubes
1 cup panko bread crumbs
1 cup crushed pretzels

1 In a medium bowl, whisk together egg, sriracha, yellow mustard and mayonnaise. Toss in chicken cubes. Refrigerate covered for 30 minutes or up to overnight.

2 Preheat air fryer at 180°C for 3 minutes.

3 In a shallow dish, combine bread crumbs and crushed pretzels. Shake excess marinade off each piece of chicken and then dredge in bread crumb mixture.

4 Add half of chicken bites to air fryer basket. Cook for 4 minutes. Shake gently. Cook for an additional 5 minutes. Check the chicken using a meat thermometer to ensure the internal temperature is at least 75°C. Repeat with remaining chicken.

5 Transfer to a plate and serve warm.

PER SERVING

KILOJOULES: 1016 | **FAT:** 6.4g | **PROTEIN:** 27.8g | **SODIUM:** 490mg | **FIBRE:** 0.4g | **CARBOHYDRATES:** 18.9g | **SUGAR:** 1.1g

Chicken Quesadillas

Due to its ability to evenly cook tortillas, the air fryer is the perfect appliance for quesadillas. These chicken quesadillas are tasty on their own but round out a meal when served with sour cream, guacamole, shredded lettuce and a side of rice and black beans.

- **Hands-On Time:** 10 minutes
- **Cook Time:** 12 minutes

Serves 4

2 medium Roma tomatoes, seeded and diced
1 teaspoon chilli powder
1/2 teaspoon salt
2 1/4 tablespoons butter, melted
8 (15cm) flour tortillas
2 cups shredded cooked chicken
2 cups grated Mexican cheese blend

1. In a small bowl, toss diced tomatoes with chilli powder and salt. Set aside.
2. Preheat air fryer at 180°C for 3 minutes.
3. Lightly brush melted butter on one side of a tortilla. Place tortilla butter side down in air fryer basket. Layer 1/4 of the shredded chicken on tortilla, followed by 1/4 of the tomatoes and 1/4 of the cheese. Top with second tortilla. Lightly butter top of tortilla.
4. Cook for 3 minutes. Set aside and continue to make three more quesadillas.
5. Slice each quesadilla like a pie into six sections. Serve warm.

PER SERVING

KILOJOULES: 2543 | **FAT:** 30.5g | **PROTEIN:** 41.5g | **SODIUM:** 967mg | **FIBRE:** 2.1g | **CARBOHYDRATES:** 33.4g | **SUGAR:** 3.6g

Chicken and Green Olive Pizzadillas

Pizza + quesadilla = pizzadilla! The interesting combination of ingredients coupled with the fresh amazing taste will make you come back for more!

- **Hands-On Time:** 10 minutes
- **Cook Time:** 12 minutes

Serves 4

2 cups shredded cooked chicken
1 teaspoon garlic powder
2 ¼ tablespoons butter, melted
8 (15cm) flour tortillas
1 cup Super Easy Romesco Sauce (see page 71)
2 cups grated mozzarella cheese
1 cup sliced pitted green olives
2 teaspoons fresh thyme leaves

1 In a small bowl, toss chicken with garlic powder.

2 Preheat air fryer at 180°C for 3 minutes.

3 Lightly brush melted butter on one side of a tortilla. Place tortilla butter side down in air fryer basket. Spread ¼ of romesco sauce on tortilla in basket. Layer ¼ of the chicken, ¼ of the cheese, ¼ of the olives and ¼ of the thyme leaves. Top with second tortilla. Lightly butter top of tortilla. Cook for 3 minutes. Set aside and continue to make the other three pizzadillas.

4 Slice each pizzadilla into six sections. Serve warm.

PER SERVING

KILOJOULES: 3029 | **FAT:** 40.5g | **PROTEIN:** 43.0g | **SODIUM:** 1,844mg | **FIBRE:** 4.3g | **CARBOHYDRATES:** 40.5g | **SUGAR:** 3.4g

Chicken Taco Bowl

Taco Tuesday just found a new recipe. Although there are mixed greens at the bottom of this loaded bowl, it is definitely a step up from a tired dinner salad.

- **Hands-On Time:** 15 minutes
- **Cook Time:** 15 minutes

Serves 4

3/4 tablespoon avocado oil
1 teaspoon chilli powder
1/2 teaspoon ground cumin
1/8 teaspoon garlic powder
1/8 teaspoon smoked paprika
1/8 teaspoon salt
Pinch cayenne pepper
450 grams boneless, skinless chicken thighs, thinly sliced into 3cm strips
4 cups mixed greens
1 cup yellow corn kernels
1 cup black beans, rinsed and drained
1 large avocado, peeled, pitted and diced
2 medium Roma tomatoes, seeded and diced
16 tortilla chips
1/2 cup sour cream

BENEFITS OF AVOCADO OIL

Avocado oil, pressed from the pulp of avocados, is touted as having positive effects on heart health by reducing blood pressure and cholesterol due to its healthy fats. And because of its moisturising oleic acid, it can also be used as a night cream after cleansing your face. Wash it off in the morning and tackle your day with glowing skin!

1. In a medium bowl, whisk together avocado oil, chilli powder, cumin, garlic powder, paprika, salt and cayenne pepper. Add chicken and toss. Refrigerate covered for 30 minutes.
2. Preheat air fryer at 180°C for 3 minutes.
3. Add chicken to air fryer basket. Cook for 6 minutes. Toss. Cook for another 6 minutes. Toss. Cook for 3 minutes more.
4. To assemble bowls, distribute mixed greens among four bowls. Top with chicken, corn, black beans, avocado and tomatoes. Crush 4 chips over each bowl. Drizzle with sour cream.

PER SERVING

KILOJOULES: 3589 | **FAT:** 60.5g | **PROTEIN:** 32.9g | **SODIUM:** 1,325mg | **FIBRE:** 9.8g | **CARBOHYDRATES:** 41.9g | **SUGAR:** 6.5g

8

Beef, Pork and Lamb Main Dishes

Chilli-Seasoned Rib-Eye Steak

Cut from the rib area, the rib eye is beautifully marbled, and because of this extra fat, the taste is amazing. Be sure to add the tablespoon of water to the bottom of the air fryer. When the fat renders down, the water will help to avoid the fat drippings from smoking.

- **Hands-On Time:** 5 minutes
- **Cook Time:** 10 minutes

Serves 2

¾ tablespoon water
½ teaspoon salt
¼ teaspoon freshly ground black pepper
¼ teaspoon garlic powder
¼ teaspoon chilli powder
¼ teaspoon smoked paprika
340 grams boneless rib-eye steak, 3cm thick
¾ tablespoon unsalted butter, cut into 2 pats

1. Preheat air fryer at 200°C for 3 minutes. Pour 1 tablespoon water into the bottom of the air fryer.
2. In a small bowl, combine salt, pepper, garlic powder, chilli powder and paprika.
3. Season rib eye on both sides with prepared dry rub. Place steak on fryer basket and cook for 5 minutes. Flip steak and cook for an additional 5 minutes. This should yield a medium-rare steak. Due to differences in steak sizes and cooking preferences, check steak with a meat thermometer to ensure it is cooked to your liking.
4. Transfer steak to a cutting board and top with two pats of butter. Let steak rest for 5 minutes before cutting and serving.

PER SERVING

KILOJOULES: 2476 | **FAT:** 46.2g | **PROTEIN:** 40.2g | **SODIUM:** 695mg | **FIBRE:** 0.3g | **CARBOHYDRATES:** 0.8g | **SUGAR:** 0.1g

IS RESTING COOKED MEAT NECESSARY?

Resting meat is absolutely necessary if you prefer a juicy and flavourful dish. It not only cools the meat, but also reabsorbs the juices, which is key. If you cut the meat immediately after removing it from the heat, the juices will just pour out onto your cutting board. Those juices help flavour and keep the meat moist.

BBQ Short Ribs

Short ribs are taken from the shorter portion of the rib cage. Full of meat and fat, they make the best bites of the ribs. Warning: this is not elegant dining, so bring a stack of serviettes!

- **Hands-On Time:** 10 minutes
- **Cook Time:** 16 minutes

Serves 2

$^1/_4$ cup tomato sauce
1 teaspoon Worcestershire sauce
$^3/_4$ tablespoon pure maple syrup
1 teaspoon apple cider vinegar
1 teaspoon garlic powder
$^3/_4$ tablespoon smoked paprika
1 teaspoon sea salt
1 teaspoon freshly ground black pepper
$^1/_2$ teaspoon cayenne pepper
450 grams boneless beef short ribs

1. In a large plastic resealable bag, combine tomato sauce, Worcestershire sauce, syrup, vinegar, garlic powder, paprika, salt, black pepper and cayenne pepper. Set aside $1^1/_2$ tablespoons of mixture in a small bowl.
2. Add short ribs to bag, seal and massage mixture into ribs. Refrigerate for 30 minutes or up to overnight.
3. Preheat air fryer at 160°C for 3 minutes.
4. Place ribs in air fryer basket. Cook for 8 minutes. Flip ribs and brush with extra sauce. Cook for an additional 8 minutes.
5. Transfer ribs to a serving plate.

PER SERVING

KILOJOULES: 1610 | **FAT:** 20.5g | **PROTEIN:** 43.5g | **SODIUM:** 534mg | **FIBRE:** 0.6g | **CARBOHYDRATES:** 7.1g | **SUGAR:** 5.1g

MEASURING MAPLE SYRUP WITHOUT THE MESS

When measuring sticky liquids like maple syrup, honey or molasses, warm up the measuring cup or spoon by rinsing it first with hot water. Your liquid won't stick to your cup, making clean-up much easier and the measurement more accurate!

Porcini-Rubbed Filets Mignons

Dried mushrooms can be found at most specialty grocers or online. Also, if you can't get your hands on porcinis, try other varieties, as they will fill in just nicely.

- **Hands-On Time:** 15 minutes
- **Cook Time:** 12 minutes

Serves 2

Porcini Dry Rub

¼ cup dried porcini mushrooms (about 14 grams)

2 teaspoons sugar

2 teaspoons salt

2 teaspoons black peppercorns

1 teaspoon smoked paprika

1 teaspoon dried minced garlic

Steak

2 (4cm-thick) eye fillet steaks (about 450 grams total)

1 tablespoon unsalted butter, cut into 2 pats

1. Place Porcini Dry Rub ingredients in a small food processor or spice grinder. Pulse until powdered. Store in an airtight container until ready to use. This makes about ½ cup, so you will have leftover dry rub for future meals.
2. Preheat air fryer at 190°C for 3 minutes.
3. Season steaks on both sides with prepared dry rub. Place steaks in fryer basket and cook for 4 minutes. Flip steaks and cook for an additional 4 minutes. Flip steaks one more time and cook for an additional 4 minutes. This should yield medium-rare steaks. Due to differences in steak sizes and cooking preferences, check steak with a meat thermometer to ensure it is cooked to your liking.
4. Transfer steaks to a cutting board and top each with a pat of butter. Let rest for 5 minutes before serving.

PER SERVING (½ CUP)

KILOJOULES: 1803 | **FAT:** 19.3g | **PROTEIN:** 56.3g | **SODIUM:** 1,304mg | **FIBRE:** 0.9g | **CARBOHYDRATES:** 5.7g | **SUGAR:** 2.3g

Beef Wellington

Beef Wellington is a beautiful filet mignon with Dijon mustard and mushroom duxelles wrapped neatly in puff pastry. You'll feel like there is a special little present on each plate.

- **Hands-On Time:** 15 minutes
- **Cook Time:** 27 minutes

Serve 2

2 cups chopped shiitake mushrooms (about 110 grams)
1/4 cup diced brown onion
3/4 tablespoon fresh thyme leaves
4 teaspoons olive oil, divided
2 (4cm-thick) eye fillet steaks (about 450 grams)
110 grams prosciutto (8 slices)
1 teaspoon Dijon mustard
1/4 cup plain flour, divided
1 large egg, whisked
1 sheet puff pastry, thawed to room temperature

WHAT ARE MUSHROOM DUXELLES?

Traditionally found in Beef Wellington, mushroom duxelles is simply a paste made up of mushrooms, shallots or onions, herbs and butter or oil. It is also amazing served at a party as an appetiser spread on toasted slices of French bread.

1. In a medium frying pan over medium-high heat, stir-fry shiitakes, onion, thyme and 2 teaspoons olive oil. Cook for 3–4 minutes until onions are translucent and moisture has released from mushrooms. Let cool. Transfer to a small food processor and pulse until smooth.
2. In the same frying pan, add remaining 2 teaspoons olive oil. Add steaks and sear all sides, for 4–5 minutes until browned. Set aside to rest.
3. On a flat, clean surface, place a large piece of plastic wrap. In the middle of the wrap overlap 4 prosciutto slices, forming a square. Spread half of mushroom mixture, or duxelles, over prosciutto. Add a steak to the centre. Brush top with 1/2 teaspoon Dijon mustard. Use the plastic wrap to help guide the prosciutto over steak, completely covering the steak. Roll tightly in the wrap and then twist ends of the wrap until a tight seal is formed. Repeat with remaining ingredients. Refrigerate for 30 minutes to help set the forms.

Beef Wellington
(continued)

4 Sprinkle some of the flour on flat, clean surface. The remaining flour can be used for your hands and the rolling pin. Place whisked egg in a small bowl nearby. Roll pastry sheet to 6mm thickness. Cut in half. Unwrap steaks and place one in the middle of each piece of puff pastry. Wrap steaks with puff pastry to cover. Cut away any excess pastry. Use egg to seal edges. Brush tops of Beef Wellingtons with egg.

5 Preheat air fryer at 180°C for 3 minutes.

6 Place Beef Wellingtons seam side down in air fryer basket and cook for 18 minutes. This should yield a medium-rare steak. Due to differences in steak sizes and cooking preferences, check steak with a meat thermometer to ensure it is cooked to your liking.

7 Transfer Beef Wellingtons to plates. Let rest for 5 minutes before serving.

PER SERVING

KILOJOULES: 3196 | **FAT:** 42.9g | **PROTEIN:** 72.8g | **SODIUM:** 477mg | **FIBRE:** 2.3g | **CARBOHYDRATES:** 18.2g | **SUGAR:** 2.4g

Summer Steak Salad

There is no need to spend big bucks at your local steakhouse, because this salad will quench your craving. Filled with succulent steak strips, bright greens, vibrant blue cheese, earthy nuts and seeds, and fresh blueberries, this salad is packed with flavour!

- **Hands-On Time:** 5 minutes
- **Cook Time:** 19 minutes

Serves 4

¼ cup olive oil
1 teaspoon salt
½ teaspoon freshly ground black pepper
1 (450 gram) flank steak
8 cups mixed greens
¼ cup balsamic vinaigrette
3 tablespoons blue cheese, crumbled
3 tablespoons walnut pieces
3 tablespoons shelled sunflower seeds
1 cup blueberries

WHY CUTTING ACROSS THE GRAIN IS IMPORTANT

In some cuts of meat, the parallel-lined muscle fibres are bigger than in other cuts of meat. To just take a big bite out of the meat, you are dealing with these fibres and chewing and chewing. If you thinly slice the meat against the grain, you are cutting these Fibres, leaving a tender piece of meat to enjoy instead of "chewing steak gum"!

1. In a medium bowl or large plastic resealable bag, combine olive oil, salt and pepper. Add flank steak, seal and toss. Refrigerate for 30 minutes or up to overnight.
2. Preheat air fryer at 160°C for 3 minutes.
3. Place steak on fryer basket and cook for 10 minutes. Flip steak and cook for an additional 9 minutes. This should yield a medium-rare steak. Due to differences in steak sizes and cooking preferences, check steak with a meat thermometer to ensure it is cooked to your liking.
4. Transfer steak to a cutting board. Let rest for 5 minutes.
5. While steak is resting, add mixed greens to a large mixing bowl. Slowly drizzle in vinaigrette. Toss. Add more and toss again. Do this until greens are fully dressed. Transfer to four bowls.
6. Top each salad with blue cheese, walnuts, sunflower seeds and blueberries.
7. Slice steak thinly across the grain for maximum tenderness. Top each salad with sliced steak. Serve immediately.

PER SERVING

KILOJOULES: 1786 | **FAT:** 26.0g | **PROTEIN:** 30.2g | **SODIUM:** 269mg | **FIBRE:** 3.7g | **CARBOHYDRATES:** 13.0g | **SUGAR:** 6.6g

Brie and Fig Jam Sliders

Break out these upscale sliders for a family celebration or for your fancy guests! Fig jam and Brie go together like peanut butter and jam. The peppery rocket leaves elevate these sliders and will have you coming back for more... and more!

- **Hands-On Time:** 5 minutes
- **Cook Time:** 89 minutes

Serves 4

450 grams lean beef mince
½ teaspoon dried basil
½ teaspoon salt
6 tablespoons Brie cheese
8 slider buns
¼ cup fig jam
½ cup rocket

1. In a medium bowl, combine beef, basil and salt. Form into eight balls.
2. Roll ¾ tablespoon of Brie into a ball and press into the middle of a beef ball. Seal edges and gently press into a patty. Gently make a slight indentation in the middle of each patty, as the beef will rise during heating. Repeat with remaining beef and Brie.
3. Preheat air fryer at 180°C for 3 minutes.
4. Place four sliders in lightly greased air fryer basket or on the air fryer grill pan (accessory). Cook for 4 minutes. Flip sliders and cook an for additional 5 minutes or until cooked to your liking, which can be checked with a meat thermometer. Repeat with remaining sliders.
5. Transfer sliders to a plate and serve on buns spread with fig jam and topped with rocket.

PER SERVING

KILOJOULES: 1882 | **FAT:** 14.8g | **PROTEIN:** 30.8g | **SODIUM:** 749mg | **FIBRE:** 1.5g | **CARBOHYDRATES:** 42.4g | **SUGAR:** 13.5g

Steak Street Tacos

Because they're overflowing with flavour, you will think these street tacos came off a gourmet food truck. Cutting the air-fried flank steak against the grain causes this cheaper cut of meat to seem like it is the highest-priced beef from the butcher.

- **Hands-On Time:** 5 minutes
- **Cook Time:** 19 minutes

Serves 4

1/4 cup olive oil
1/2 teaspoon salt
1/2 teaspoon ground cumin
1 (450 gram) flank steak
10 street tacos (10 cm mini flour tortillas)
1 cup shredded red cabbage
1/2 cup Sriracha Mayonnaise **(see page 72)**
1/2 cup Pico Guacamole **(see page 68)**

1. In a large plastic resealable bag, combine olive oil, salt and cumin. Add flank steak, seal and toss. Refrigerate for 30 minutes.
2. Preheat air fryer at 160°C for 3 minutes.
3. Place steak on fryer basket and cook for 10 minutes. Flip steak and cook for an additional 9 minutes. This should yield a medium-rare steak. Due to differences in steak sizes and cooking preferences, check steak with a meat thermometer to ensure it is cooked to your liking.
4. Transfer steak to a cutting board. Let rest for 5 minutes before cutting. Slice thinly against the grain for maximum tenderness.
5. Build street tacos by adding steak slices to flour tortillas, along with red cabbage, sriracha mayonnaise and pico guacamole. Serve immediately.

PER SERVING

KILOJOULES: 2200 | **FAT:** 33.7g | **PROTEIN:** 24.2g | **SODIUM:** 739mg | **FIBRE:** 3.5g | **CARBOHYDRATES:** 26.0g | **SUGAR:** 3.1g

Hamburger Dogs

Turn the classic hamburger and hot dog on their heads by combining the two. This hot dog is actually seasoned beef mince in the shape of a hot dog and served in a hot dog bun. You can serve them with your favourite burger or hot dog toppings.

- **Hands-On Time:** 5 minutes
- **Cook Time:** 6 minutes

Serves 4

230 grams beef mince
1/4 teaspoon Worcestershire sauce
1 large egg white
1 1/2 tablespoons plain bread crumbs
1/8 teaspoon chilli powder
1/4 teaspoon onion powder
1/4 teaspoon salt
4 top-split hot dog buns

1 In a medium bowl, combine beef, Worcestershire sauce, egg white, bread crumbs, chilli powder, onion powder and salt. Form into four hot dog shapes. Roll them longer than usual because the beef will shrink a bit in cooking.

2 Preheat air fryer at 180°C for 3 minutes.

3 Place hamburger dogs in lightly greased air fryer basket. Cook for 3 minutes. Flip. Cook for an additional 3 minutes. Transfer to a paper towel–lined plate to soak up any grease.

4 Place hamburger dogs in buns and serve.

PER SERVING

KILOJOULES: 887 | **FAT:** 5.1g | **PROTEIN:** 14.8g | **SODIUM:** 423mg | **FIBRE:** 1.1g | **CARBOHYDRATES:** 23.7g | **SUGAR:** 3.0g

Bulgogi

Bulgogi, literally translated as "fire meat", is a Korean classic consisting of thin strips of marinated beef. The air fryer makes crispy edges on the beef strips, which lend added texture to this dish. The grated pear is the secret weapon and quintessential ingredient in Bulgogi.

- **Hands-On Time:** 15 minutes
- **Cook Time:** 12 minutes

Serves 2

1 ½ tablespoons sesame oil
1 ½ tablespoons grated pear
¾ tablespoon soy sauce
¾ tablespoon brown sugar
¾ tablespoon gochujang
1 teaspoon ground ginger
1 clove garlic, minced
Pinch salt
6 spring onions, trimmed, sliced, whites and greens separated
1 (340 gram) rib-eye steak, 3cm thick, thinly sliced
2 cups cooked rice
2 teaspoons toasted sesame seeds

1. In a large plastic resealable bag, combine oil, pear, soy sauce, sugar, gochujang, ginger, garlic, salt and spring onion whites. Add thinly sliced rib eye, seal and toss. Refrigerate for 30 minutes or up to overnight.
2. Preheat air fryer at 190°C for 3 minutes.
3. Place steak in air fryer basket and cook for 12 minutes, stirring every 3 minutes. This should yield tender steak with crispy edges.
4. Serve steak over two bowls of rice. Garnish with spring onion greens and toasted sesame seeds.

PER SERVING

KILOJOULES: 2623 | **FAT:** 30.0g | **PROTEIN:** 38.0g | **SODIUM:** 208mg | **FIBRE:** 1.1g | **CARBOHYDRATES:** 47.8g | **SUGAR:** 1.4g

Reuben Burgers

These burgers have all the classic flavours of a Reuben sandwich coupled with the juiciness of the simple hamburger. The air-fried corned beef takes the place of crispy bacon found on some burgers, and the caraway seeds give a nod to the traditional rye bread.

- **Hands-On Time:** 10 minutes
- **Cook Time:** 30 minutes

Serves 4

450 grams lean beef mince
1 ½ tablespoons brown onion, finely chopped
2 teaspoons caraway seeds
1 teaspoon salt
4 slices Swiss cheese
8 slices deli corned beef
½ cup Thousand Island dressing
4 hamburger buns
1 cup sauerkraut, drained

1. Preheat air fryer at 180°C for 3 minutes.
2. Combine beef mince, onion, caraway seeds and salt. Form into four patties, making an indentation in the middle, as the beef will rise during heating.
3. Add two patties to lightly greased fryer basket and cook for 6 minutes. Flip burgers and cook for an additional 4 minutes. Add a slice of Swiss cheese to the top of the burgers and cook for an additional 2 minutes.
4. Transfer to a serving plate. Repeat with remaining burgers. Remove when done and let them rest.
5. While burgers are resting, add corned beef to air fryer basket. Cook for 3 minutes, flip and cook for an additional 3 minutes to achieve crispy edges.
6. Spread 1½ tablespoons dressing on each bun. Place a burger on each bun and top each with ¼ cup sauerkraut and 2 slices crispy corned beef. Serve warm.

PER SERVING

KILOJOULES: 2313 | **FAT:** 25.9g | **PROTEIN:** 45.1g | **SODIUM:** 1,529mg | **FIBRE:** 2.8g | **CARBOHYDRATES:** 32.9g | **SUGAR:** 9.2g

Hoisin Beef Meatballs

Hoisin has an incredibly rich flavour, hitting both sweet and salty tastes. These are fantastic straight out of the air fryer but even better served over rice garnished with scallion greens and eaten with a pair of chopsticks.

- **Hands-On Time:** 10 minutes
- **Cook Time:** 16 minutes

Serves 4

450 grams lean beef mince
1 large egg
½ cup panko bread crumbs
4 spring onions trimmed and diced, greens and whites separated
1 ½ tablespoons hoisin sauce
¾ tablespoon soy sauce
½ teaspoon ground white pepper

1. Preheat air fryer at 180°C for 3 minutes.
2. In a medium bowl, combine beef, egg, bread crumbs, white parts of spring onions, hoisin sauce, soy sauce and pepper. Form into 18 meatballs, about 2 tablespoons each.
3. Add half of meatballs to fryer basket and cook for 6 minutes. Flip meatballs. Cook for an additional 2 minutes. Transfer to serving dish.
4. Repeat with remaining meatballs.
5. Transfer meatballs to a serving dish. Garnish with spring onion greens.

WHAT IS WHITE PEPPER?

White and black pepper are not only different in colour, they are also different in flavour and preparation. Black pepper is made from berries that aren't ripe but are smoked, creating a black colour. White pepper is created from ripe berries by removing the skin and soaking the berries. Removing the skin removes some of the flavour, which is why black pepper has a deeper flavour. White pepper is more subtle and is also good for white sauces, where the black pepper would inconveniently show itself.

PER SERVING

KILOJOULES: 1112 | **FAT:** 10.0g | **PROTEIN:** 25.1g | **SODIUM:** 420mg | **FIBRE:** 0.5g | **CARBOHYDRATES:** 14.4g | **SUGAR:** 2.9g

Red Wine Beef

Although this meal is simply made, the Dijon mustard and red wine lend a little acidic bite that will be appreciated with the robust beef. Serve with potatoes and green beans.

- **Hands-On Time:** 5 minutes
- **Cook Time:** 15 minutes

Serves 4

1 teaspoon Dijon mustard
1/2 teaspoon salt
1/4 cup dry red wine
1/4 cup tomato paste
450 grams beef stew cubes

WHAT KIND OF WINE SHOULD YOU BUY FOR COOKING?

If a recipe calls for dry red wine, using a red blend or a Merlot, Cabernet, Pinot Noir or Shiraz will all fit the bill. The best rule for you as chef is to choose a wine that you enjoy to drink. Because you won't be using the entire bottle, there are leftovers for the cook, so buy what you like! Or if you don't like wine, vegetable or chicken broth is a good substitute for white wine and beef broth can substitute for red wine.

1 In a medium bowl, combine mustard, salt, wine and tomato paste. Add in beef cubes and toss to combine. Add to bottom of cake barrel (accessory).
2 Preheat air fryer at 180°C for 3 minutes.
3 Place barrel in air fryer basket. Cook for 12–15 minutes, stirring twice during cooking.
4 Remove barrel from air fryer and let rest for 10 minutes. Spoon into bowls and serve warm.

PER SERVING

KILOJOULES: 991 | **FAT:** 7.2g | **PROTEIN:** 25.2g | **SODIUM:** 396mg | **FIBRE:** 0.7g | **CARBOHYDRATES:** 3.6g | **SUGAR:** 2.1g

Simple Pork Loin Roast

The air fryer definitely does justice to a succulent pork loin roast. The interior meat is so very juicy, and the convection-style cooking does wonders to crisp up the skin. Because of varying sizes of loin roasts, be sure to check the roast with a meat thermometer near the end of the cooking cycle.

- **Hands-On Time:** 10 minutes
- **Cook Time:** 40 minutes

Serves 4

1 (910 gram) boneless pork loin roast
3 cloves garlic, halved
¾ tablespoon olive oil
1 teaspoon dried rosemary
1 teaspoon salt
½ teaspoon freshly ground black pepper

1. Preheat air fryer at 180°C for 3 minutes.
2. Cut six random slits, about 3cm deep, in top of pork loin. Push a garlic half in each slit.
3. In a small bowl, whisk together olive oil, rosemary, salt and pepper. Massage into loin on all sides.
4. Place pork in air fryer basket. Cook for 20 minutes. Flip. Cook for 20 minutes more. The internal temperature should be at least 70°C when checked with a meat thermometer.
5. Let pork rest on a cutting board for 5 minutes before slicing and serving warm.

PER SERVING

KILOJOULES: 1857 | **FAT:** 23.2g | **PROTEIN:** 42.5g | **SODIUM:** 713mg | **FIBRE:** 0.2g | **CARBOHYDRATES:** 0.4g | **SUGAR:** 0.0g

Parmesan-Crusted Pork Chops

The Parmesan cheese coating sets these air-fried pork chops apart from any others. Done in 12 minutes, they can rest while you plate the rest of your food. By the time the plate makes it to the table, they will be ready to eat!

- **Hands-On Time:** 5 minutes
- **Cook Time:** 12 minutes

Serves 2

1 large egg
3/4 tablespoon Dijon mustard
1/4 cup grated Parmesan cheese
1/4 cup panko bread crumbs
1/4 teaspoon freshly ground black pepper
2 (3cm-thick) bone-in pork chops, approximately 450 grams

WHY DO CHICKEN EGGS COME IN DIFFERENT SIZES AND COLOURS?

Most grocery stores typically sell chicken eggs ranging from small to jumbo. And white and brown eggs are the colours you generally see, but sometimes eggs are bluish or greenish. These variations all come down to the breed and age of the hen. Where you really get a different flavour is not necessarily from the size of the egg or age of the hen, but from the freshness, the way the chicken was raised and the quality of its diet.

1 Preheat air fryer at 180°C for 3 minutes.

2 In a small dish, whisk together egg and Dijon mustard. In a shallow dish combine Parmesan cheese, bread crumbs and black pepper.

3 Dip pork chops in egg mixture. Coat in bread crumb mixture.

4 Place pork on lightly greased air fryer basket. Cook for 4 minutes. Flip. Cook for 4 minutes more. Flip. Cook for an additional 4 minutes. The internal temperature should be at least 70°C when checked with a meat thermometer.

5 Let pork rest on a cutting board for 5 minutes before serving warm.

PER SERVING

KILOJOULES: 376 | **FAT:** 17.8g | **PROTEIN:** 34.3g | **SODIUM:** 425mg | **FIBRE:** 0.1g | **CARBOHYDRATES:** 12.3g | **SUGAR:** 0.6g

Pork Schnitzel

Pork schnitzel, or *Schweineschnitzel*, is pork cutlet that has been pounded thin and breaded. The air fryer cooks all sides to a tasty crispness. Serve this schnitzel with your favourite potato dish for a complete German dining experience.

- **Hands-On Time:** 15 minutes
- **Cook Time:** 42 minutes

Makes 6 schnitzels

6 boneless pork loin steaks
1/2 cup plain flour
1 large egg, whisked
1 cup panko bread crumbs
3/4 tablespoon ground dry mustard
1 teaspoon freshly ground black pepper
1 1/2 tablespoons lemon juice
2 teaspoons salt
1 medium lemon, cut into 6 wedges

THE DIFFERENCE BETWEEN SCHNITZEL AND WIENER SCHNITZEL

Schnitzel is simply the cooking preparation of pounding meat until thin, crumbing it and lightly frying it. Wiener schnitzel is still prepared this way, but it is always veal. Other popular versions are *Jägerschnitzel*, which is schnitzel served with a mushroom gravy, and *Rahmschnitzel*, which is served with a cream sauce.

1. Place a loin between two pieces of baking paper. Using the flat side of a mallet, pound out pork until it is 3mm thick. Repeat with remaining loins. Set aside.
2. In a small bowl, add flour. In another bowl, add whisked egg. In a shallow dish, combine bread crumbs, ground mustard and black pepper.
3. Preheat air fryer at 180°C for 3 minutes.
4. Sprinkle each loin with lemon juice and salt on both sides.
5. Coat each loin in flour. Shake off excess. Dip in egg and shake off excess. Coat in bread crumbs.
6. Place pork on lightly greased air fryer basket. Cook for 4 minutes. Flip. Cook for 3 minutes. Repeat with remaining pork. The internal temperature should be at least 70°C when checked with a meat thermometer.
7. Let pork rest on a cutting board 5 minutes before serving warm with lemon wedges.

PER SERVING

KILOJOULES: 652 | **FAT:** 3.4g | **PROTEIN:** 19.7g | **SODIUM:** 852mg | **FIBRE:** 0.3g | **CARBOHYDRATES:** 11.3g | **SUGAR:** 0.5g

Crispy Teriyaki Pork and Rice

By thinly slicing the pork prior to cooking, you allow the air fryer to give those delicious crispy edges to this succulent meat, which adds another dimension of flavour and texture to this simple dish.

- **Hands-On Time:** 10 minutes
- **Cook Time:** 17 minutes

Serves 4

450 grams pork shoulder, trimmed and thinly sliced into thin 3cm-long strips
1/2 cup plus 3/4 tablespoon teriyaki sauce
1 1/2 tablespoons water
3/4 tablespoon honey
2 cups cooked rice
1/4 cup chopped fresh coriander

1. In a medium bowl, add pork and 1/2 cup teriyaki sauce. Refrigerate covered for 30 minutes.
2. Preheat air fryer at 180°C for 3 minutes. Add water to bottom of air fryer.
3. Place pork in air fryer basket. Cook for 5 minutes. Toss. Cook for 6 minutes more. Toss. Cook for an additional 6 minutes.
4. In a small bowl, whisk together 3/4 tablespoon teriyaki sauce and honey. Toss cooked pork in sauce.
5. Serve pork over cooked rice and garnish with coriander.

PER SERVING

KILOJOULES: 1464 | **FAT:** 13.4g | **PROTEIN:** 23.4g | **SODIUM:** 909mg | **FIBRE:** 0.4g | **CARBOHYDRATES:** 30.1g | **SUGAR:** 7.5g

Sweet and Sour Pork

As an added component to this dish, use the pineapple juice from a can of pineapple chunks. Then toss the chunks in the sauce with the pork at the end of this recipe. Serve the mixture over rice to complete the take-out experience... and don't forget to buy those fortune cookies!

- **Hands-On Time:** 15 minutes
- **Cook Time:** 20 minutes

Serves 4

2 ¹⁄₄ tablespoons cornflour, divided
³⁄₄ tablespoon water
1 ¹⁄₂ tablespoons rice vinegar
1 ¹⁄₂ tablespoons tomato sauce
¹⁄₃ cup pineapple juice
1 ¹⁄₂ tablespoons brown sugar
2 teaspoons soy sauce
1 large egg
1 ¹⁄₂ tablespoons plain flour
450 grams boneless pork loin, cut into 3cm cubes

CORNFLOUR SUBSTITUTIONS

Cornflour is an ingredient used to thicken such things as sauces and puddings. It is also sometimes used in frying, as it can lend a crispier crumb. However, if you have run out of it or have certain diet restrictions, the following can be used — flour, arrowroot flour, tapioca flour, rice flour and even potato starch.

1. In a small bowl, create a slurry by whisking together 1 tablespoon cornflour and water. Set aside.
2. In a small saucepan over medium heat, combine rice vinegar, tomato sauce, pineapple juice, sugar and soy sauce. Cook for 3 minutes, stirring continuously. Add cornflour slurry and heat for 1 more minute. Set pan away from heat and allow to thicken.
3. In a medium bowl, whisk together egg, flour and the remaining cornflour.
4. Preheat air fryer at 180°C for 3 minutes.
5. Dip pork cubes in egg batter. Shake off any excess.
6. Add pork in two batches to air fryer basket. Cook for 4 minutes. Shake gently. Cook for an additional 4 minutes. Check the pork using a meat thermometer to ensure the internal temperature is at least 75°C.
7. Transfer to a bowl. Add sauce and toss until coated. Serve warm.

PER SERVING

KILOJOULES: 949 | **FAT:** 4.1g | **PROTEIN:** 24.5g | **SODIUM:** 291mg | **FIBRE:** 0.3g | **CARBOHYDRATES:** 20.5g | **SUGAR:** 10.7g

Spaghetti and Meatballs

Cooking the meatballs in the air fryer basket before coating them with the napoletana sauce allows them to get a sear on the exterior before bathing in the aromatic napoletana! Top with grated Parmesan cheese and fresh parsley, and there will be no confusion why this is a staple on so many family tables.

- **Hands-On Time:** 15 minutes
- **Cook Time:** 16 minutes

Serves 4

450 grams dry spaghetti
450 grams pork mince
1 large egg
¼ cup chopped fresh basil
2 cloves garlic, minced
½ teaspoon salt
¼ cup plain bread crumbs
2 cups napoletana sauce
3 tablespoons grated Parmesan cheese
¼ cup chopped fresh parsley

1. Cook spaghetti according to packet directions.
2. Preheat air fryer at 180°C for 3 minutes.
3. In a medium bowl, combine pork, egg, basil, garlic, salt and bread crumbs. Form into 16 meatballs, about 2 tablespoons each.
4. Add eight meatballs to fryer basket and cook for 6 minutes. Transfer to cake barrel (accessory). Repeat with remaining eight meatballs. Pour napoletana sauce over meatballs. Place cake barrel with all the meatballs in air fryer basket. Cook for an additional 4 minutes.
5. Distribute spaghetti evenly among four bowls. Top each with meatballs and sauce. Garnish with Parmesan cheese and fresh parsley. Serve warm.

PER SERVING

KILOJOULES: 2782 | **FAT:** 8.6g | **PROTEIN:** 43.4g | **SODIUM:** 797mg | **FIBRE:** 5.3g | **CARBOHYDRATES:** 96.1g | **SUGAR:** 7.2g

Beer Bratwurst

This German classic just clamours to be served with your favourite potato dish and a little spicy mustard to drag your bratwurst through. If you are opposed to using beer in this recipe, substitute beef broth and a dash or two of Worcestershire sauce. It will be equally as delicious!

- **Hands-On Time:** 15 minutes
- **Cook Time:** 21 minutes

Serves 4

450 grams uncooked pork bratwurst
1 (375ml) bottle or can of beer
2 cups water
½ medium brown onion, peeled and sliced

1 Pierce each bratwurst two times with the tines of a fork. Add to a medium saucepan with beer, water and onion. Bring to a boil. Reduce heat and simmer for 15 minutes. Drain.

2 Preheat air fryer at 200°C for 3 minutes.

3 Place bratwurst and onions in fryer basket. Cook for 3 minutes. Flip and cook for an additional 3 minutes. Check with a meat thermometer to ensure an internal temperature of 75°C.

4 Transfer bratwurst and onions to a plate and serve warm.

PER SERVING

KILOJOULES: 1292 | **FAT:** 24.8g | **PROTEIN:** 12.6g | **SODIUM:** 767mg | **FIBRE:** 0.2g | **CARBOHYDRATES:** 4.0g | **SUGAR:** 0.6g

Pork Lettuce Cups

This seems like a long list of ingredients, but once you make this recipe, you'll want to make it over and over again. You'll just have to replenish the fresh ingredients each time. The bottled ingredients will be on hand already!

- **Hands-On Time:** 10 minutes
- **Cook Time:** 40 minutes

Serves 6

1/2 cup rice vinegar
1/4 cup sugar
Pinch salt
1 large carrot, peeled and julienned
1 medium English cucumber, peeled and diced
1 spring onion, trimmed and diced
1 (910 gram) boneless pork loin roast
1 teaspoon salt
1/2 teaspoon freshly ground black pepper
1/4 cup soy sauce
1 1/2 tablespoons honey
3/4 tablespoon sriracha
2 teaspoons fish sauce
1 teaspoon ground ginger
1 teaspoon ground white pepper
12 Butter lettuce leaves
1/2 cup chopped fresh basil

1. In a medium bowl, whisk together vinegar, sugar and salt. Add carrot, cucumber and spring onion. Toss to coat and refrigerate covered until ready to use.
2. Preheat air fryer at 180°C for 3 minutes.
3. Season roast with salt and black pepper.
4. Place pork in air fryer basket. Cook for 20 minutes. Flip. Cook for 20 minutes more. The internal temperature should be at least 70°C when checked with a meat thermometer.
5. Let pork rest on a cutting board for 5 minutes, then shred pork using two forks.
6. In a large bowl, whisk together soy sauce, honey, sriracha, fish sauce, ginger and white pepper. Add in sliced pork and toss to fully coat.
7. Assemble lettuce cups by adding an equal portions of coated pork to the centre of each lettuce leaf. Top with vegetable mixture and garnish with fresh basil.

PER SERVING

KILOJOULES: 1460 | **FAT:** 17.2g | **PROTEIN:** 29.2g | **SODIUM:** 1,286mg | **FIBRE:** 1.1g | **CARBOHYDRATES:** 14.0g | **SUGAR:** 11.7g

BBQ Pork Bowl

Pork, barbecue sauce, fresh corn and mashed potatoes — if there is a way to someone's heart through their stomach, these four ingredients combined should do the trick!

- **Hands-On Time:** 15 minutes
- **Cook Time:** 20 minutes

Serves 4

1 pound pork shoulder, trimmed and thinly sliced into 3cm-long strips
½ cup barbecue sauce of your choice
1 ½ tablespoons water
1 cup corn kernels
2 large Russet potatoes, peeled and diced into 6mm cubes
1 ½ tablespoons butter
¼ cup full-cream milk
1 teaspoon salt
1 teaspoon freshly ground black pepper
¼ cup chopped fresh parsley

KITCHEN HACK: OBTAINING FRESH CORN KERNELS

Using an angel food or Bundt pan, place corn on its end in the centre of the pan. Using a sharp knife, gently cut down the sides of the corn. The kernels will catch in the pan. Afterward, take a butter knife and run it down the cob to get that fresh "milk." That juice adds flavour you don't want to miss.

1 In a medium bowl, add pork and barbecue sauce. Refrigerate covered for 30 minutes.

2 Preheat air fryer at 180°C for 3 minutes. Add water to bottom of air fryer.

3 Place pork in air fryer basket. Cook for 6 minutes. Toss. Cook for 6 minutes more. Add corn and toss. Cook for an additional 3 minutes.

4 While pork is cooking, add potatoes to a pot of boiling salted water and cook for 4–5 minutes until fork-tender. Drain potatoes and transfer to a medium bowl. Add butter, milk, salt and pepper. Mash until smooth.

5 Serve pork and corn over mashed potatoes and garnish with fresh parsley.

PER SERVING

KILOJOULES: 1702 | **FAT:** 19.6g | **PROTEIN:** 23.4g | **SODIUM:** 1,026mg | **FIBRE:** 2.8g | **CARBOHYDRATES:** 32.1g | **SUGAR:** 9.7g

Rack of Lamb with Mint Pesto

Fresh pesto can make anything taste good. And this minty variation on the classic basil pesto pairs naturally with a fancy rack of lamb. This dish is guest-worthy if you are trying to impress and sexy enough for a dinner for two.

- **Hands-On Time:** 10 minutes
- **Cook Time:** 25 minutes

Serves 2

1 1/2 cups fresh parsley
1 1/2 cups fresh mint leaves
1/3 cup pine nuts
4 cloves garlic, halved
3/4 cup freshly grated Parmesan cheese
3-4 tablespoons olive oil
Pinch salt
1 (8-rib) Frenched rack of lamb (about 680 grams)
1/2 teaspoon salt
1/2 teaspoon freshly ground black pepper

WHAT IS A FRENCHED RACK OF LAMB?

Frenching a rack of lamb is simply removing that fat and cartilage from the small end of the rib bones. It creates a more visually appealing look to your final product. It is pretty easy to do on your own, especially with the assistance of a *YouTube* video, but just ask your butcher. He or she would be happy to clean up your lamb.

1. In a food processor, pulse parsley, mint and pine nuts. Add garlic, Parmesan cheese and 1 tablespoon olive oil. Pulse again. Slowly add remaining oil until desired consistency. Add a pinch salt. Transfer to a jar and refrigerate. Pesto can be made the night before.
2. Season lamb with salt and pepper.
3. Preheat air fryer at 120°C for 3 minutes.
4. Add lamb to fryer basket and cook for 20 minutes. Increase temperature to 200°C and cook for an additional 5 minutes. Use a meat thermometer to ensure that the meat is at least 48°C.
5. Transfer lamb to a cutting board, wrap in aluminium foil and let rest for 10 minutes, which will increase the temperature to 63°C, yielding a medium-rare cook.
6. Slice between the ribs and serve warm with mint pesto.

PER SERVING

KILOJOULES: 5481 | **FAT:** 99.7g | **PROTEIN:** 67.4g | **SODIUM:** 1,532mg | **FIBRE:** 4.1g | **CARBOHYDRATES:** 16.2g | **SUGAR:** 1.3g

Moroccan Lamb Pizza

Talk about a twist! The tahini on this unique pizza acts as the sauce. Topped with Moroccan-spiced lamb, pine nuts and fresh herbs, your taste buds will be working overtime. The creamy goat cheese is mild enough to let all of those flavours shine.

- **Hands-On Time:** 15 minutes
- **Cook Time:** 39 minutes

Serves 4

110 grams lamb mince
1/2 medium red onion, peeled and diced
2 cloves garlic, minced
1/2 teaspoon ground cardamom
1/2 teaspoon ground ginger
1/4 teaspoon ground cinnamon
3 tablespoons tahini
3/4 tablespoon lemon juice
1/2 teaspoon salt
230 grams fresh pizza dough (about the size of a tennis ball)
1/2 cup goat cheese, crumbled
1 1/2 tablespoons chopped fresh mint
1 1/2 tablespoons chopped fresh parsley
2 teaspoons pine nuts

1. In a medium frying pan over medium-high heat, stir-fry lamb, onion, garlic, cardamom, ginger and cinnamon. Cook 4–5 minutes until lamb is browned. Set aside.
2. In a small bowl, combine tahini, lemon juice and salt. Set aside.
3. Preheat air fryer at 95°C for 6 minutes.
4. Press out half of dough to fit pizza pan (accessory). Cook for 7 minutes.
5. Turn up heat to 140°C.
6. Remove basket and spread half of tahini mixture over dough, leaving a 6mm outer crust uncovered. Add half of lamb mixture. Cook for an additional 10 minutes.
7. Gently transfer pizza to a cutting board. Add half of goat cheese, mint, parsley and pine nuts.
8. Repeat making pizza with remaining ingredients. Serve warm.

MAKES 2 PERSONAL PIZZAS

KILOJOULES: 3447 | **FAT:** 44.1g | **PROTEIN:** 37.8g | **SODIUM:** 1,550mg | **FIBRE:** 5.8g | **CARBOHYDRATES:** 66.4g | **SUGAR:** 8.7g

Garlic-Rosemary Lamb Loin Chops

There is no need to overcomplicate these little lamb chops, as they are so flavourful.

- **Hands-On Time:** 5 minutes
- **Cook Time:** 9 minutes

Serves 3

1/4 cup olive oil
2 teaspoons lemon juice
4 cloves garlic, minced
1 teaspoon salt
1/4 teaspoon freshly ground black pepper
4 sprigs fresh rosemary
3 lamb loin chops, each approximately 3cm thick (about 450 grams total)

FRESH LEMON JUICE VERSUS BOTTLED LEMON JUICE

So let's say it all together: fresh is *always* the best choice. As with anything on a shelf, bottled lemon juice is going to have preservatives. Case in point, here are the ingredients in a lemon juice bottle: lemon juice from concentrate (water, concentrated lemon juice), sodium benzoate, sodium metabisulfite, sodium sulfite (preservatives) and lemon oil. The other drawback of bottled lemon juice is that they don't have any zest.

1. In a shallow dish, whisk together oil, lemon juice, garlic, salt and pepper. Add rosemary sprigs and lamb. Refrigerate covered for 30 minutes.
2. Preheat air fryer at 190°C for 3 minutes.
3. Add lamb chops to fryer basket and cook for 5 minutes. Flip chops and cook for an additional 4 minutes. Use a meat thermometer to ensure that the meat is at least 63°C.
4. Transfer to a cutting board and let rest for 5 minutes. Serve warm.

MAKES 2 PERSONAL PIZZAS

KILOJOULES: 1744 | **FAT:** 24.6g | **PROTEIN:** 41.0g | **SODIUM:** 695mg | **FIBRE:** 0.1g | **CARBOHYDRATES:** 1.3g | **SUGAR:** 0.1g

Greek Lamb Burgers

These are a fun twist on the classic American burger. The lamb mince is mixed with traditional Greek flavours, such as red onion, garlic, mint, dill and olives.

- **Hands-On Time:** 10 minutes
- **Cook Time:** 24 minutes

Serves 4

450 grams lamb mince
1 ½ tablespoons red onion, finely chopped
¾ tablespoon minced Kalamata olives
2 cloves garlic, minced
1 large egg white
¼ cup panko bread crumbs
2 teaspoons dried mint
2 teaspoons dried dill
Pinch salt
4 thick slices large tomato

1. Preheat air fryer at 180°C for 3 minutes.
2. In a medium bowl, combine lamb, onion, olives, garlic, egg white, bread crumbs, mint, dill and salt. Form into four patties, making a slight indentation in the middle of each patty.
3. Add two patties to lightly greased fryer basket and cook for 6 minutes. Flip burgers and cook for an additional 6 minutes or until cooked to your liking when checked with a meat thermometer. Repeat with remaining burgers.
4. Transfer to a plate and serve warm with a thick slice of tomato on each burger.

PER SERVING

KILOJOULES: 1230 | **FAT:** 16.9g | **PROTEIN:** 23.6g | **SODIUM:** 167mg | **FIBRE:** 0.6g | **CARBOHYDRATES:** 7.5g | **SUGAR:** 1.2g

Fish and Seafood Main Dishes

Parmesan Fish Fingers

Cod and pollack are the typical fishes used in traditional fish fingers. But when making this recipe, feel free to try salmon, sea bass or other firm, flaky fish that is fresh at your seafood counter. Serve these fish fingers with your favourite dipping sauce.

- **Hands-On Time:** 10 minutes
- **Cook Time:** 20 minutes

Serves 4

½ cup plain flour
1 large egg, whisked
½ cup panko bread crumbs, crushed fine
½ cup grated Parmesan cheese
450 grams cod, cut into 3cm sticks

PARMESAN CHEESE: FRESH OR GRATED?

There really isn't a huge taste difference between shredded cheese and the hunks of cheese you grate yourself. The big difference is in how you use it. With the fresh chunk of cheese, you are able to either grate it on some meals or use a vegetable slicer to peel slices for other meals. Pasta and salads are lovely places to showcase those beautiful Parmesan cheese curls.

1. Add flour to a small bowl. Add egg to another small bowl. Add bread crumbs and Parmesan cheese to a shallow dish.
2. Preheat air fryer at 180°C for 3 minutes.
3. Roll fish fingers in flour. Shake off excess flour. Dip in whisked egg. Shake off excess egg. Roll in bread crumb mixture. Remove to a plate.
4. Add half of fish fingers to fryer basket. Cook for 5 minutes. Carefully flip fish fingers. Cook for an additional 5 minutes. Repeat with remaining fish.
5. Transfer fish fingers to a serving plate and serve warm.

PER SERVING

KILOJOULES: 669 | **FAT:** 2.4g | **PROTEIN:** 20.7g | **SODIUM:** 468mg | **FIBRE:** 0.2g | **CARBOHYDRATES:** 11.9g | **SUGAR:** 0.3g

Crab Cakes

For a fancy brunch, top these crab delicacies with a poached egg and silky hollandaise sauce and delight in your eggs Benedict upgrade! Or serve with your preferred dipping sauce.

- **Hands-On Time:** 15 minutes
- **Cook Time:** 10 minutes

Serves 4

450 grams lump crabmeat, picked over and any shells discarded
⅓ cup mayonnaise
1 teaspoon Dijon mustard
1 teaspoon lemon juice
¾ tablespoon brown onion, finely chopped
½ cup crushed Ritz crackers
1 ½ tablespoons chopped fresh parsley
1 large egg
1 teaspoon Old Bay Seasoning
Pinch salt

1. In a medium bowl, carefully combine crabmeat, mayonnaise, mustard, lemon juice, onion, cracker crumbs, parsley, egg, Old Bay Seasoning and salt. Form mixture into eight patties.
2. Preheat air fryer at 200°C for 3 minutes.
3. Place patties in lightly greased air fryer basket. Cook for 5 minutes. Flip crab cakes. Cook for an additional 5 minutes.
4. Transfer to a serving dish and let rest for 5 minutes before serving warm.

PER SERVING

KILOJOULES: 1209 | **FAT:** 17.5g | **PROTEIN:** 22.9g | **SODIUM:** 1,068mg | **FIBRE:** 0.3g | **CARBOHYDRATES:** 7.0g | **SUGAR:** 1.1g

CHOOSING CRABMEAT

Fresh lump crabmeat is the best option for this recipe — but it can be pricey. Fortunately, there are many different varieties and sections of the crab that can be purchased at a lower price point. Crab is even sold in cans like the more familiar tuna. Although there is imitation "krab" available, draw the line at that. It is stringy and packed with starch and chemicals.

Salmon Patties with Apple Salsa

This recipe calls for canned salmon for ease; however, leftover cooked salmon or freshly cooked salmon flaked into pieces are perfectly viable options.

- **Hands-On Time:** 20 minutes
- **Cook Time:** 10 minutes

Serves 4

Apple Salsa

½ cup diced red onion
½ cup seeded and diced red capsicum
1 small Granny Smith apple, peeled, cored and diced
¾ tablespoon chopped fresh dill
Juice of 1 small lime
Pinch salt

Salmon Patties

410 grams canned wild-caught salmon
½ cup mayonnaise
1 large egg
1 ½ tablespoons seeded red capsicum, finely chopped
½ cup panko bread crumbs
Pinch salt

THERE ARE BONES IN MY CANNED SALMON!

The cooking and canning process for canned salmon makes these bones soft and edible, and they are an excellent source of calcium. This same theory goes for sardines. You eat the whole fish, right? You can also eat the bones in canned salmon.

1. In a small bowl, combine apple salsa ingredients. Refrigerate covered until ready to use.
2. In a medium bowl, combine salmon, mayonnaise, egg, capsicum, bread crumbs and salt. Form mixture into eight salmon patties.
3. Preheat air fryer at 200°C for 3 minutes.
4. Place in lightly greased air fryer basket. Cook for 5 minutes. Flip salmon patties. Cook for an additional 5 minutes.
5. Transfer to a serving dish and let rest for 5 minutes before serving warm with apple salsa.

PER SERVING

KILOJOULES: 2020 | **FAT:** 27.6g | **PROTEIN:** 36.6g | **SODIUM:** 771mg | **FIBRE:** 1.4g | **CARBOHYDRATES:** 18.5g | **SUGAR:** 5.9g

Curried Prawn Cakes

When choosing prawns for these cakes, don't worry about the size of the prawn, because they will be finely chopped. Fresh prawns are best but thawed frozen prawns are also an option.

- **Hands-On Time:** 15 minutes
- **Cook Time:** 20 minutes

Serves 4

450 grams raw prawns, peeled, deveined and finely chopped
1/4 cup seeded and finely diced red capsicum
3/4 tablespoon red curry paste
3 cloves garlic, minced
1 teaspoon lime juice
3/4 tablespoon shallot, finely chopped
1/2 cup panko bread crumbs
1 large egg
1 1/2 tablespoons mayonnaise
1 teaspoon grated fresh ginger
Pinch salt
1 cup diced fresh mango, peeled
1/4 cup chopped fresh Thai basil (or regular basil)
1 large lime, cut into 8 wedges

1. In a medium bowl, combine prawns, capsicum, curry, garlic, lime juice, shallot, bread crumbs, egg, mayonnaise, ginger and salt. Form into eight prawn cakes.
2. Preheat air fryer at 200°C for 3 minutes.
3. Place four prawn cakes in lightly greased air fryer basket. Cook for 5 minutes. Flip prawn cakes. Cook for an additional 5 minutes. Repeat with remaining cakes.
4. Transfer to a serving plate. Garnish with diced mango and chopped basil. Serve warm with lime wedges.

PER SERVING

KILOJOULES: 974 | **FAT:** 7.7g | **PROTEIN:** 19.5g | **SODIUM:** 870mg | **FIBRE:** 1.1g | **CARBOHYDRATES:** 20.1g | **SUGAR:** 7.0g

WHAT IS THAI BASIL?

Thai basil has a purple stem and is stronger in flavour than the traditional Italian basil found in most grocery stores simply labelled "basil". The varieties have different taste and aroma profiles, and some chefs say they are interchangeable in a recipe.

Lobster Tails

If those live lobster tanks give you the heebie-jeebies and prevent you from cooking lobster at home, you're probably not alone. But most supermarkets or fish mongers sell little tails weighing between 140-170 grams in the seafood section, which makes handling this elegant meat much easier.

- **Hands-On Time:** 10 minutes
- **Cook Time:** 8 minutes

Serves 2

2 (140-150 gram) small uncooked lobster tails
3/4 tablespoon butter, melted
1/2 teaspoon Old Bay Seasoning
3/4 tablespoon chopped fresh parsley
2 lemon wedges

MAKING BROTH WITH LOBSTER TAIL SHELLS

Don't discard those empty lobster tail shells. You can make a beautiful broth for lobster bisque, crab soup or a seafood gumbo. Place the shells in a Dutch oven or heavy-bottomed pot with 4 cups water, 1 peeled and diced brown onion, 1 peeled and diced carrot, 1 diced celery stalk and 2 peeled, halved garlic cloves. Bring to boil. Reduce heat and simmer covered for 30 minutes. Use a slotted spoon to remove and discard the solids from the broth. Strain the remaining liquid through a fine-mesh sieve or cheesecloth. Cover broth and refrigerate for up to 4 days or freeze for up to 6 months.

1. Using kitchen shears, cut down the middle of each lobster tail on the softer side. Carefully run your finger between the lobster meat and the soft underside of the shell to loosen meat.
2. Preheat air fryer at 200°C for 3 minutes.
3. Place tails in air fryer basket, cut side up. Cook for 4 minutes. Brush with butter and sprinkle with Old Bay Seasoning. Cook for an additional 3–4 minutes, depending on the size of the lobster tail.
4. Serve warm garnished with parsley and lemon wedges.

PER SERVING

KILOJOULES: 715 | **FAT:** 6.4g | **PROTEIN:** 25.9g | **SODIUM:** 800mg | **FIBRE:** 0.1g | **CARBOHYDRATES:** 0.1g | **SUGAR:** 0.1g

Cornflake-Crusted Cod

The cornflakes give this fish an unconventional crust, and the horseradish mustard gives it a delightful contrasting sharpness. Serving this dish with a creamy sauce brings it home!

- **Hands-On Time:** 10 minutes
- **Cook Time:** 10 minutes

Serves 2

½ cup crushed cornflakes
1 teaspoon dried dill
⅛ teaspoon salt
¾ tablespoon horseradish mustard
1 teaspoon lemon juice
¾ tablespoon butter, melted
2 (170 gram) cod fillets

1. In a small bowl, combine cornflakes, dill, salt, mustard, lemon juice and butter.
2. Preheat air fryer at 180°C for 3 minutes.
3. Press the cornflake mixture evenly across the top of the cod fillets. Place fish in lightly greased air fryer basket.
4. Cook for 10 minutes or until fish is opaque and flakes easily with a fork. Cooking times may vary due to size and thickness of fillets.
5. Transfer to serving plates and serve warm.

PER SERVING

KILOJOULES: 1158 | **FAT:** 6.9g | **PROTEIN:** 32.6g | **SODIUM:** 571mg | **FIBRE:** 0.7g | **CARBOHYDRATES:** 17.9g | **SUGAR:** 2.0g

Seared Sea Scallops

The convection oven-style of cooking in the air fryer sears these scallops beautifully on all sides. Serve the scallops with steamed asparagus, mashed potatoes and a drizzle of fresh hollandaise sauce over everything for decadent bites of yummy!

- **Hands-On Time:** 5 minutes
- **Cook Time:** 8 minutes

Serves 2

1 ½ tablespoons butter, melted
¾ tablespoon fresh lemon juice
450 grams jumbo sea scallops (about 10)

1. Preheat air fryer at 200°C for 3 minutes.
2. In a small bowl, combine butter and lemon juice. Roll scallops in mixture to coat all sides.
3. Place scallops in air fryer basket. Cook for 2 minutes. Flip scallops. Cook for 2 minutes more. Brush the tops of each scallop with butter mixture. Cook for 2 minutes. Flip scallops. Cook for an additional 2 minutes.
4. Transfer scallops to a serving plate and serve warm.

PER SERVING

KILOJOULES: 1062 | **FAT:** 11.4g | **PROTEIN:** 28.1g | **SODIUM:** 909mg | **FIBRE:** 0.0g | **CARBOHYDRATES:** 7.9g | **SUGAR:** 10.2g

Baked Ling with Blood Orange Aioli

Although the more readily available navel orange can be used as a substitute in this recipe, the gorgeous red-fleshed blood orange not only lends colour but flavour with its berry undertones.

- **Hands-On Time:** 10 minutes
- **Cook Time:** 10 minutes

Serves 2

1/4 cup mayonnaise
1 teaspoon Dijon mustard
1 teaspoon fresh blood orange zest
4 teaspoons fresh blood orange juice
3/4 teaspoon salt, divided
2 (170 gram) ling fillets
1/2 teaspoon freshly ground black pepper
1 tablespoon chopped fresh chives

1. In a small bowl, whisk together mayonnaise, Dijon mustard, orange zest, orange juice and 1/4 teaspoon salt. Refrigerate covered until ready to use.
2. Preheat air fryer at 180°C for 3 minutes.
3. Season ling fillets with 1/2 teaspoon salt and pepper.
4. Place ling in lightly greased air fryer basket. Cook for 10 minutes or until fish is opaque and flakes easily with a fork. Cooking times may vary due to size and thickness of fillets.
5. Transfer to serving plates and serve warm with blood orange aioli. Garnish with chives.

PER SERVING

KILOJOULES: 1472 | **FAT:** 22.2g | **PROTEIN:** 32.2g | **SODIUM:** 1,224mg | **FIBRE:** 0.3g | **CARBOHYDRATES:** 2.0g | **SUGAR:** 1.1g

Macadamia-Crusted Barramundi with Horseradish-Lemon Aioli

The buttery and decadent barramundi coupled with the buttery and creamy nature of macadamia nuts makes this a double threat. Served with tangy horseradish-lemon aioli, this dish makes a five-star meal.

- **Hands-On Time:** 10 minutes
- **Cook Time:** 12 minutes

Serves 2

1 ½ tablespoons crushed salted macadamia nuts
1 ½ tablespoons panko bread crumbs
1 teaspoon horseradish mustard
1 teaspoon lime juice
¾ tablespoon butter, melted
2 (170 gram) barramundi fillets
2 tablespoons Horseradish-Lemon Aioli (see page 72)

1 In a small bowl, combine macadamia nuts, bread crumbs, mustard, lime juice and butter.
2 Preheat air fryer at 180°C for 3 minutes.
3 Press the nut mixture evenly across the tops of the barramundi. Place fish in lightly greased air fryer basket.
4 Cook for 12 minutes, ensuring that the barramundi is opaque and flakes easily with a fork.
5 Transfer to serving plates and serve warm with horseradish-lemon aioli on the side.

PER SERVING

KILOJOULES: 1535 | **FAT:** 21.4g | **PROTEIN:** 33.1g | **SODIUM:** 257mg | **FIBRE:** 0.8g | **CARBOHYDRATES:** 6.8g | **SUGAR:** 0.8g

Coconut Prawns

The simple approach to this recipe highlights the sweetness of the coconut crust and allows the prawns to shine. Choose a fun dipping sauce to enjoy with this dish.

- **Hands-On Time:** 10 minutes
- **Cook Time:** 8 minutes

Serves 2

1/3 cup plain flour
1 1/2 tablespoons cornflour
1 teaspoon salt
1/4 cup whole milk
1 large egg
1/4 cup panko bread crumbs
1/2 cup sweetened shredded coconut
230 grams (about 40) medium raw prawns, tail on, deveined and shelled

1. In a medium bowl, combine flour, cornflour and salt.
2. In another medium bowl, whisk together milk and egg.
3. In a shallow dish, combine bread crumbs and coconut.
4. Preheat air fryer at 190°C for 3 minutes.
5. Toss prawns in flour mixture. Coat in egg mixture and then dip in bread crumb mixture. Shake off excess at each step.
6. Place prawns in lightly oiled air fryer basket. Cook for 4 minutes. Gently flip prawns. Cook for an additional 4 minutes.
7. Transfer prawns to a plate and serve warm.

PER SERVING

KILOJOULES: 1715 | **FAT:** 12.3g | **PROTEIN:** 24.8g | **SODIUM:** 1,978mg | **FIBRE:** 1.7g | **CARBOHYDRATES:** 47.0g | **SUGAR:** 12.2g

Tuna Croquettes

When you don't have salmon on hand, open a few cans of tuna for an old-fashioned meal with a modern twist using your air fryer. Creamy and crunchy and filled with nutrition, these tuna croquettes are a great lunch or an addition atop a light salad.

- **Hands-On Time:** 15 minutes
- **Cook Time:** 12 minutes

Serves 4

425 gram can tuna in spring water, drained
1/3 cup mayonnaise
1 teaspoon lemon juice
1/4 teaspoon Worcestershire sauce
3/4 tablespoon red onion, finely chopped
1/2 cup crushed panko bread crumbs
1 1/2 tablespoons chopped fresh parsley
1 large egg
1/2 teaspoon ground mustard
Pinch salt
1/4 teaspoon freshly ground black pepper
1 medium lime, cut into 6 wedges

1. In a medium bowl, combine tuna, mayonnaise, lemon juice, Worcestershire sauce, onion, bread crumbs, parsley, egg, mustard, salt and pepper. Form mixture into 16 croquettes approximately 2 tablespoons each, which are similar to a large potato tot with rounded ends.
2. Preheat air fryer at 200°C for 3 minutes.
3. Place eight croquettes in lightly greased air fryer basket. Cook for 3 minutes. Flip croquettes. Cook for an additional 3 minutes. Transfer to a serving plate. Repeat with remaining croquettes.
4. Squeeze lime over croquettes. Enjoy warm with preferred sauce.

PER SERVING

KILOJOULES: 1476 | **FAT:** 21.5g | **PROTEIN:** 26.0g | **SODIUM:** 539mg | **FIBRE:** 0.2g | **CARBOHYDRATES:** 10.9g | **SUGAR:** 0.9g

Beer-Battered Calamari Rings

Calamari can be found in the frozen section of your store, sometimes cut into circles; however, fresh squid tubes can usually be purchased at the fish counter and are easy to slice. The flavour of this recipe can be changed simply by swapping out the kind of beer you use. Serve them with your favourite dipping sauce.

- **Hands-On Time:** 15 minutes
- **Cook Time:** 8 minutes

Serves 4

1/2 cup beer
1/4 cup plain flour
1 cup panko bread crumbs
1 teaspoon salt
1/2 teaspoon freshly ground black pepper
150 grams (about 6) calamari tubes, cut into 6 rings per tube
1/4 cup chopped fresh parsley
1 medium lime, quartered

1. In a small bowl, whisk together beer and flour.
2. In a shallow dish, combine bread crumbs, salt and pepper.
3. Preheat air fryer at 200°C for 3 minutes.
4. Coat the calamari rings in beer mixture. Shake off excess. Roll all of the rings through bread crumb mixture.
5. Place half of the calamari rings in lightly greased air fryer basket. Cook for 2 minutes. Flip calamari. Cook for an additional 2 minutes. Transfer to a serving dish and repeat with remaining calamari.
6. Garnish with parsley and lime quarters.

PER SERVING

KILOJOULES: 422 | **FAT:** 0.9g | **PROTEIN:** 7.9g | **SODIUM:** 336mg | **FIBRE:** 0.3g | **CARBOHYDRATES:** 14.6g | **SUGAR:** 0.5g

Crab-Stuffed John Dory Roulade

This mouth-watering and succulent crab-stuffed John Dory roulade is a beautiful dish to serve when entertaining. Plus, let's be honest, crab is dreamy in anything you serve!

- **Hands-On Time:** 15 minutes
- **Cook Time:** 6 minutes

Serves 4

4 (140 gram) John Dory fillets

½ cup lump crabmeat, picked over and any shells discarded

2 teaspoons mayonnaise

1 teaspoon horseradish mustard

½ teaspoon chopped fresh dill

1 large egg

1 ½ tablespoons water

1 cup panko bread crumbs

1 teaspoon salt

½ teaspoon freshly ground black pepper

1 ½ tablespoons butter, melted

4 lime wedges

1. Between two pieces of baking paper, gently pound John Dory fillets until "rollable", about 6mm thickness.
2. In a small bowl, combine crab, mayonnaise, horseradish mustard and dill.
3. In a separate small bowl, whisk together egg and water.
4. In a shallow dish, combine bread crumbs, salt and pepper.
5. Preheat air fryer at 180°C for 3 minutes.
6. Divide crab mixture among fillets and spread evenly. Tightly and gently roll a fillet from one short end to the other. Secure with a toothpick. Repeat with each fillet.
7. Roll each fillet in egg mixture and coat in bread crumb mixture.
8. Place fish in lightly greased air fryer basket. Drizzle tops with melted butter. Cook for 6 minutes.
9. Transfer to a serving dish and let rest for 5 minutes. Remove toothpicks. Serve warm with lime wedges.

PER SERVING

KILOJOULES: 1008 | **FAT:** 10.2g | **PROTEIN:** 23.1g | **SODIUM:** 888mg | **FIBRE:** 0.1g | **CARBOHYDRATES:** 10.3g | **SUGAR:** 0.5g

Fried Sardines

There's no need for an egg dip with this crumb, as the olive oil gives enough slickness for the bread crumbs to adhere. For a flavour boost, purchase sardines already marinated in mustard or napoletana sauce, then follow this recipe per usual!

- **Hands-On Time:** 5 minutes
- **Cook Time:** 6 minutes

Serves 2

½ cup panko bread crumbs
2 (110 gram) cans skinless, boneless sardines in pure olive oil, drained
2 lemon wedges

WHY YOU SHOULD GIVE SARDINES A TRY

You either love or loathe sardines. To some, they just seem weird. But, sardines are packed with nutrition. Plus, crumbing them and giving them a whirl in the air fryer takes some of the visual scary away. Sardines are not only tasty but also loaded with omega-3 fatty acids, vitamin D, protein and selenium. And as a bonus they are economical and low in mercury and other metals.

1. Preheat air fryer at 180°C for 3 minutes.
2. Place bread crumbs in a shallow dish. Roll sardines to coat with bread crumbs.
3. Place in lightly greased air fryer basket. Cook for 3 minutes. Gently flip sardines and cook for an additional 3 minutes.
4. Serve warm with lemon wedges..

PER SERVING

KILOJOULES: 1020 | **FAT:** 12.3g | **PROTEIN:** 18.5g | **SODIUM:** 354mg | **FIBRE:** 0.0g | **CARBOHYDRATES:** 15.0g | **SUGAR:** 0.8g

Vegetarian and Vegan Dishes

Tofu Tikka Masala over Turmeric Rice

Tikka masala is a gorgeous purée of tomatoes, cream and spices such as cinnamon, cardamom, nutmeg, coriander, peppercorns and more. The tofu takes on these flavours and adds protein.

- **Hands-On Time:** 10 minutes
- **Cook Time:** 8 minutes

Serves 2

230 grams extra-firm tofu, cut into 6mm cubes
½ medium brown onion, peeled and thinly sliced
½ cup jarred tikka masala, divided
1 teaspoon coconut oil
2 cloves garlic, minced
2 teaspoons ground turmeric
½ cup basmati rice
1 cup vegetable broth
¼ cup chopped fresh coriander

1. In a medium bowl, combine cubed tofu, onion and ¼ cup tikka masala. Toss to coat.
2. In a medium saucepan, heat coconut oil over medium heat until melted. Add garlic and sauté for 1 minute. Add turmeric, rice and broth. Bring to a boil. Reduce heat and simmer covered for 15 minutes.
3. Preheat air fryer at 180°C for 3 minutes.
4. Place tofu mixture into air fryer basket. Cook for 4 minutes. Shake. Cook for an additional 4 minutes. Transfer to a medium bowl and toss with remaining ¼ cup tikka masala.
5. Spoon rice into two bowls. Top with tofu. Garnish with coriander and serve warm.

PER SERVING

KILOJOULES: 1447 | **FAT:** 8.9g | **PROTEIN:** 13.5g | **SODIUM:** 550mg | **FIBRE:** 3.5g | **CARBOHYDRATES:** 51.9g | **SUGAR:** 5.5g

TURMERIC 101

Turmeric is the main ingredient in several Indian curry dishes, but it is also what gives that yellow Spanish rice its beautiful golden hue. This aromatic spice filled with notes of ginger and citrus adds a depth of flavour to many dishes. Its original form is a root, which can be handled similarly to ginger root. Turmeric is said to stimulate digestion, reduce inflammation and even help boost brain health.

Tofu Buddha Bowl

Buddha bowls are all the rage these days. Packed with vegetables, beans, tofu, quinoa and rocket, this bowl is overflowing with flavours, texture and nutrition. The heartiness of the ingredients will ensure that you stay full and satisfied for many hours.

- **Hands-On Time:** 10 minutes
- **Cook Time:** 16 minutes

Serves 4

1/2 small brown onion, peeled and sliced
1 cup peeled, diced sweet potato (6mm cubes)
1 teaspoon avocado oil
230 grams extra-firm tofu, cut into 6mm cubes
1 cup canned chickpeas, drained and rinsed
1/2 teaspoon five spice powder
1/2 teaspoon chilli powder
1/4 teaspoon salt
2 teaspoons fresh lime zest
1 cup cooked quinoa
2 cups rocket
2 medium carrots, peeled and shredded
1 medium avocado, peeled, pitted and diced

1. In a medium bowl, combine onion, sweet potato and avocado oil.
2. In another bowl, combine tofu, chickpeas, five spice powder, chilli powder and salt.
3. Preheat air fryer at 180°C for 3 minutes.
4. Place onion mixture into lightly greased air fryer basket. Cook for 8 minutes. Add tofu mixture to onion mixture. Stir. Cook for an additional 8 minutes.
5. Stir lime zest into cooked quinoa.
6. Prepare four Buddha bowls by evenly distributing rocket, carrots, avocado, quinoa and tofu mixture among the bowls. Serve immediately.

PER SERVING

KILOJOULES: 1054 | **FAT:** 8.3g | **PROTEIN:** 10.8g | **SODIUM:** 308mg | **FIBRE:** 8.3g | **CARBOHYDRATES:** 33.6g | **SUGAR:** 6.0g

Rice Bowl with Cauliflower and Tahini Aioli

This complex bowl of flavour contains rice mixed with wilted spinach leaves and topped with seasoned air-fried cauliflower florets. A drizzle of the tahini aioli ties everything together.

- **Hands-On Time:** 15 minutes
- **Cook Time:** 8 minutes

Serves 4

Tahini Aioli

1/4 cup tahini
1 1/2 tablespoons Veganaise
1 teaspoon dried coriander
3/4 tablespoon tamari
1/2 teaspoon honey
2 teaspoons lime juice

Rice Bowl

4 cups cauliflower florets (about 1 small head)
3/4 tablespoon coconut oil, melted
3/4 tablespoon ground turmeric
1/4 teaspoon salt
1/4 teaspoon ground white pepper
Pinch cayenne pepper
Pinch ground cinnamon
2 cloves garlic, minced
4 cups cooked rice
2 cups baby spinach

1. In a medium bowl, whisk together tahini aioli ingredients. Refrigerate covered until ready to use.
2. Add cauliflower florets to a large bowl. Toss with coconut oil, turmeric, salt, white pepper, cayenne pepper, ground cinnamon and garlic until evenly coated.
3. Preheat air fryer at 180°C for 3 minutes.
4. Place cauliflower in air fryer basket. Cook for 4 minutes. Toss cauliflower. Cook for an additional 4 minutes.
5. Divide rice among four bowls. Add spinach leaves. Top with cooked cauliflower and toss to wilt spinach. Drizzle with prepared tahini aioli. Serve immediately.

PER SERVING

KILOJOULES: 1803 | **FAT:** 16.1g | **PROTEIN:** 10.1g | **SODIUM:** 502mg | **FIBRE:** 5.2g | **CARBOHYDRATES:** 57.0g | **SUGAR:** 3.2g

Shepherdless Pie

Loaded with vegetables and plant based mince, this shepherdless pie delivers all the punch that meat eaters get from their version. The rich filling is topped with creamy and cheesy mashed potatoes. For a different decorative effect, pipe those mashed potatoes in dollops on top before cooking.

- **Hands-On Time:** 15 minutes
- **Cook Time:** 21 minutes

Serves 4

Potato Topping

1 large potato, scrubbed and diced

3/4 tablespoon avocado oil

1/4 cup non-dairy Cheddar shreds

1 1/2 tablespoons unsweetened almond milk

1/2 teaspoon salt

1/2 teaspoon freshly ground black pepper

Meatless Filling

2 teaspoons avocado oil

1 cup plant-based mince

1/2 small brown onion, peeled and diced

1 medium carrot, peeled and diced

1/4 cup seeded and diced green capsicum

1 small celery stalk, diced

2/3 cup tomato sauce

1 teaspoon chopped fresh rosemary

1 teaspoon fresh thyme leaves

1/2 teaspoon salt

1/2 teaspoon freshly ground black pepper

1. Add diced potatoes to a medium pot of boiling salted water and cook until fork-tender for 4–5 minutes.
2. While potatoes are cooking, add 2 teaspoons avocado oil, plant-based mince, onion, carrot, capsicum and celery to a large frying pan. Cook over medium-high heat for 3–4 minutes until vegetables are tender. Stir in tomato sauce, rosemary, thyme, 1/2 teaspoon salt and 1/2 teaspoon black pepper.
3. Drain potatoes and transfer to a medium bowl. Add 1 tablespoon avocado oil, Cheddar shreds, almond milk, 1/2 teaspoon salt and 1/2 teaspoon pepper. Mash until smooth.
4. Preheat air fryer at 180°C for 3 minutes.
5. Spoon meatless filling into lightly greased round cake barrel (accessory). Top with mashed potatoes. Using a fork, run shallow lines in the top of the potatoes for a decorative touch.
6. Cook for 12 minutes. Remove barrel from air fryer and let rest for 10 minutes. Serve warm.

PER SERVING

KILOJOULES: 681 | **FAT:** 8.7g | **PROTEIN:** 6.5g | **SODIUM:** 1,065mg | **FIBRE:** 4.0g | **CARBOHYDRATES:** 16.3g | **SUGAR:** 3.5g

Fried Avocado Tacos

The crumbed avocado fries are amazingly crisp on the outside and divinely smooth on the inside. Topped with the crunchy slaw, the fresh salsa and the creamy kick from the sriracha mayonnaise, these fried avocado tacos will quickly become a household favourite.

- **Hands-On Time:** 10 minutes
- **Cook Time:** 10 minutes

Serves 2

Sriracha Mayonnaise

½ cup Veganaise
2 teaspoons sriracha
1 teaspoon lime juice
Pinch salt

Salsa

2 medium Roma tomatoes, seeded and diced
¼ cup finely diced red onion
¾ tablespoon fresh lime juice
1 teaspoon fresh lime zest
¼ cup chopped fresh cilantro
1 teaspoon salt

Avocado Fries

1 medium avocado
Egg substitute equaling 1 large egg
1 ½ tablespoons unsweetened almond milk
1 cup plain bread crumbs

Remaining Taco Ingredients

6 (15cm) flour tortillas
1 cup coleslaw mix (shredded cabbage and carrots)

1. In a small bowl, combine sriracha mayonnaise ingredients and refrigerate covered until ready to use.
2. In a medium bowl, combine salsa ingredients and refrigerate covered until ready to use.
3. Cut avocado in half. Remove pit. Use a soup spoon to gently scrape the avocado away from the skin. Gently slice each half into six "fries".
4. Whisk together egg substitute and almond milk in a small bowl. Put bread crumbs in a shallow dish.
5. Preheat air fryer at 190°C.
6. Dip avocado slices in egg mixture. Coat in bread crumbs to coat. Place half of avocado slices into air fryer basket. Cook for 5 minutes. Transfer to serving plate. Repeat with remaining avocado slices.
7. Add two fried avocado slices to each tortilla. Top with coleslaw mix, salsa and a squeeze of sriracha mayonnaise.

PER SERVING

KILOJOULES: 3589 | **FAT:** 51.7g | **PROTEIN:** 14.9g | **SODIUM:** 2,560mg | **FIBRE:** 10.3g | **CARBOHYDRATES:** 80.1g | **SUGAR:** 10.0g

Black Bean and Couscous Burgers

Whether you are vegan or a meat lover, you'll agree that these black bean burgers are just good! Both the couscous and black beans are full of nutrients. The creamy treenut cheese not only lends flavour but also acts as a binder in these patties. Serve as is or on a bun with your favourite toppings!

- **Hands-On Time:** 10 minutes
- **Cook Time:** 6 minutes

Serves 4

1/3 cup water
3/4 tablespoon plus 1/2 teaspoon olive oil, divided
1 teaspoon salt, divided
1/3 cup wholemeal couscous
1 cup canned black beans, drained and rinsed
1 1/2 tablespoons finely chopped onion
1 1/2 tablespoons chopped fresh parsley
1/4 teaspoon chipotle chilli powder
1 1/2 tablespoons creamy treenut cheese

1. In a small saucepan, bring water, 1/2 teaspoon olive oil and 1/2 teaspoon salt and bring to a boil. Remove from heat and stir in couscous. Cover and let rest for 5 minutes.
2. In a medium bowl, mash black beans. Add cooked couscous, onion, parsley, chilli powder, remaining salt and treenut cheese. Form into four patties.
3. Preheat air fryer at 180°C for 3 minutes.
4. Place patties in lightly greased air fryer basket. Cook for 3 minutes. Flip. Brush patties with remaining tablespoon olive oil. Cook for an additional 3 minutes.
5. Transfer to a plate and serve warm.

PER SERVING

KILOJOULES: 761 | **FAT:** 52.5g | **PROTEIN:** 7.0g | **SODIUM:** 754mg | **FIBRE:** 5.4g | **CARBOHYDRATES:** 22.1g | **SUGAR:** 0.6g

WHAT IS TREENUT CHEESE?

Treenut cheese is a non-dairy, gluten-free and non-GMO cheese that is an excellent choice for vegans and those affected by gluten and/or dairy. Made from cashews, acidophilus cultures and seasonings, this creamy cheese is great as a binder in these burgers and as a spread on crackers.

Beet Falafel

Falafel is traditionally a fried ball of ground chickpeas and spices. Almost like a Middle Eastern fritter, if you will. The addition of beets in this variation lends an earthiness and sweetness that makes these falafels irresistible! Try dipping them in Tzatziki Sauce (see page 75).

- **Hands-On Time:** 10 minutes
- **Cook Time:** 40 minutes

Serves 4

430 grams can chickpeas, rinsed and drained
1 cup sliced cooked beets
2 cloves garlic, minced
¼ cup spelt flour
¾ tablespoon dried coriander
½ teaspoon ground ginger
½ teaspoon salt
¼ teaspoon ground white pepper
¼ cup chopped fresh parsley

1. In a medium bowl, mash chickpeas and beets. Stir in garlic, flour, coriander, ginger, salt and pepper. Form into 20 balls.
2. Preheat air fryer at 180°C for 3 minutes.
3. Place six balls in lightly greased pizza pan (accessory) and place in air fryer basket. Cook for 5 minutes. Flip. Cook for an additional 5 minutes. Repeat with remaining balls.
4. If they have flattened in the cooking process, re-form into ball shapes when cool enough to handle. Continue to cool for another 2–3 minutes and garnish with parsley before serving.

PER SERVING

KILOJOULES: 569 | **FAT:** 1.4g | **PROTEIN:** 6.3g | **SODIUM:** 454mg | **FIBRE:** 6.2g | **CARBOHYDRATES:** 24.3g | **SUGAR:** 4.9g

Corn Fritters

Served as a snack or side dish, these corn fritters are amazing. The polenta in the crumb lends a little rustic flair and adds to the corn theme in these crispy little nuggets. Serve with your favourite dipping sauce for even more flavour!

- **Hands-On Time:** 10 minutes
- **Cook Time:** 10 minutes

Serves 3

1/2 cup corn kernels
1/4 cup seeded and finely diced red capsicum
1/2 cup grated zucchini
2 cloves garlic, minced
1/4 cup polenta
1/4 cup plain bread crumbs
1 tablespoon plain flour
1/2 teaspoon salt
1/2 teaspoon freshly ground black pepper
1 1/2 tablespoons vegetable oil
1 1/2 tablespoons water

1. In a medium bowl, combine corn, capsicum, zucchini, garlic, cornmeal, bread crumbs, flour, salt, black pepper, vegetable oil and water. Form into nine balls.
2. Preheat air fryer at 180°C for 3 minutes.
3. Place the balls in lightly greased pizza pan (accessory) and place in air fryer basket. Cook for 5 minutes. Flip. Cook for an additional 5 minutes.
4. Let cool 2–3 minutes before serving.

PER SERVING

KILOJOULES: 769 | **FAT:** 7.4g | **PROTEIN:** 3.7g | **SODIUM:** 459mg | **FIBRE:** 2.1g | **CARBOHYDRATES:** 25.6g | **SUGAR:** 3.3g

Vegetable Spring Rolls

Stuffed with cabbage, carrots, mushrooms, spring onions and bamboo shoots, and flavoured with sesame oil, garlic, soy sauce, sriracha and ginger, these vegetable spring rolls will rival the ones on any take-out menu, minus the deep-frying grease!

- **Hands-On Time:** 20 minutes
- **Cook Time:** 33 minutes

Serves 6

3/4 tablespoon sesame oil
450 gram bag coleslaw mix
1/2 cup diced mushrooms
2 spring onions, trimmed and diced
2 cloves garlic, minced
225 gram can sliced bamboo shoots, drained
1 1/2 tablespoons soy sauce
3/4 tablespoon sriracha
1/2 teaspoon ground ginger
1/4 teaspoon salt
1/4 teaspoon ground white pepper
18 spring-roll wrappers
1 1/2 tablespoons avocado oil

1. In a large frying pan over medium-high heat, drizzle sesame oil. Add coleslaw mix, mushrooms, spring onions, garlic, bamboo shoots, soy sauce, sriracha, ginger, salt and pepper. Stir-fry for 5–6 minutes until cabbage is wilted and tender.
2. Drape a damp towel over the stack of spring-roll wrappers. Place one spring-roll wrapper on a cutting board. Place approximately 1/4 cup vegetable mixture in a line in the middle of the wrapper. Fold 1cm of two opposite sides of the spring roll toward the middle. Roll ends to form a spring roll and place seam side down on a plate. Repeat with remaining wrappers.
3. Preheat air fryer at 160°C for 3 minutes.
4. Place a third of the spring rolls in the air fryer basket. Cook for 3 minutes. Lightly brush the tops of spring rolls with avocado oil. Cook for an additional 6 minutes. Repeat with remaining spring rolls.
5. Transfer to a serving plate. Serve warm.

PER SERVING

KILOJOULES: 694 | **FAT:** 7.1g | **PROTEIN:** 4.8g | **SODIUM:** 593mg | **FIBRE:** 3.2g | **CARBOHYDRATES:** 21.3g | **SUGAR:** 3.9g

Roasted Garlic

Great mixed in with mashed potatoes, hummus and even just spread on bread, roasted garlic is magic, turning whatever it touches into gold!

- **Hands-On Time:** 10 minutes
- **Cook Time:** 45 minutes

Serves 8

3 teaspoons olive oil
2 garlic bulbs, unpeeled, with top 6mm cut off
Pinch salt

1. Preheat air fryer at 200°C for 3 minutes.
2. Drizzle olive oil over garlic bulbs and rub it in with your finger. Season with a pinch of salt on each. Roll each bulb up in a square of aluminium foil.
3. Place wrapped garlic bulbs in air fryer basket. Cook for 45 minutes.
4. Unwrap each bulb. When cooled, squeeze roasted garlic from each clove and use as desired.

PER SERVING

KILOJOULES: 117 | **FAT:** 1.7g | **PROTEIN:** 0.6g | **SODIUM:** 19mg | **FIBRE:** 0.2g | **CARBOHYDRATES:** 3.0g | **SUGAR:** 0.1g

Crunchy Tortilla Strips

If you want to avoid the greasy, deep-fried version of chips, the air fryer helps achieve these crisp little tortilla strips. Fantastic on fresh salads and homemade soups.

- **Hands-On Time:** 5 minutes
- **Cook Time:** 4 minutes

Serves 8

2 (15cm) corn tortillas
3/4 tablespoon avocado oil
2 teaspoons lime juice
1/2 teaspoon salt
1/4 teaspoon freshly ground black pepper

1. Cut each tortilla in half. Slice into 1cm strips.
2. Preheat air fryer at 200°C for 3 minutes.
3. In a small bowl, whisk together avocado oil and lime juice. Brush mixture over both sides of tortilla strips. Toss with salt and pepper.
4. Place strips in air fryer basket. Cook for 2 minutes. Shake strips. Cook for an additional 2 minutes.
5. Transfer chips to a bowl to cool.

PER SERVING

KILOJOULES: 238 | **FAT:** 3.7g | **PROTEIN:** 0.7g | **SODIUM:** 295mg | **FIBRE:** 0.8g | **CARBOHYDRATES:** 5.7g | **SUGAR:** 0.2g

Napoletana Pizza Tarts

Puff pastry has been deemed vegan, but stay away from the "butter puff" variety. And vegan cheese has come a long way since its inception. It not only tastes like "real" cheese, but it does in fact melt, lending that ooey-gooey mouthfeel you are used to with traditional mozzarella cheese.

- **Hands-On Time:** 15 minutes
- **Cook Time:** 18 minutes

Serves 3

1/4 cup plain flour

1 sheet puff pastry, thawed to room temperature

1/2 cup Napoletana Sauce (see page 66)

1 (85g) meatless Italian sausage, cut into 30 slices

1/4 cup non-dairy mozzarella shreds

2 medium Roma tomatoes, cut into 12 slices

1/2 cup julienned fresh basil leaves

2 teaspoons olive oil

2 teaspoons balsamic vinegar

1. Scatter flour over a flat, clean surface. Unfold puff pastry sheet on the floured surface. Cut into six equal rectangles.
2. Top each rectangle with napoletana sauce, sausage and mozzarella shreds.
3. Preheat air fryer at 180°C for 3 minutes.
4. Place two tarts at a time in lightly greased air fryer basket. Cook for 6 minutes. Repeat with remaining tarts.
5. Top tarts with 2 slices tomato each and equal portions of basil. Lightly drizzle with oil and balsamic vinegar. Serve warm.

PER SERVING

KILOJOULES: 853 | **FAT:** 12.8g | **PROTEIN:** 7.6g | **SODIUM:** 468mg | **FIBRE:** 2.8g | **CARBOHYDRATES:** 15.6g | **SUGAR:** 3.1g

Tex-Mex Bowl

Everything you like in a taco can be found in this filling and nutritious bowl. It's quick and easy to make on a busy weeknight, and the air fryer gives the beans and corn a little crispy texture, complementing the flavour of the dish. And don't forget to make the Crunchy Tortilla Strips (see recipe on page 177)!

- **Hands-On Time:** 5 minutes
- **Cook Time:** 5 minutes

Serves 4

1 cup vegan or non-dairy sour cream
1 1/2 tablespoons unsweetened almond milk
1 teaspoon ground cumin
1 teaspoon chilli powder
Pinch cayenne pepper
1/2 teaspoon salt
1 cup canned black beans, drained and rinsed
1 cup canned corn, drained
4 cups mixed greens
3 medium Roma tomatoes, seeded and diced
1 medium avocado, peeled, pitted and diced
Crunchy Tortilla Strips (see page 177)

1. In a medium bowl, combine sour cream, almond milk, cumin, chilli powder, cayenne pepper and salt. Refrigerate covered until ready to use.
2. Preheat air fryer at 180°C for 3 minutes.
3. Place black beans and corn in air fryer basket and cook for 5 minutes.
4. Distribute mixed greens among four bowls. Top with black beans, corn, tomatoes, avocado and whole crunchy tortilla strips. Drizzle sour cream mixture over salad bowls and serve immediately.

PER SERVING

KILOJOULES: 1309 | **FAT:** 19.3g | **PROTEIN:** 6.8g | **SODIUM:** 980mg | **FIBRE:** 12.8g | **CARBOHYDRATES:** 32.9g | **SUGAR:** 1.9g

MAKING HOMEMADE ALMOND MILK IS EASIER THAN YOU THINK

Soak unsalted raw almonds covered in water for at least 24 hours. Rinse and drain. In a blender or food processor, pulse 1 3/4 cups water and 1 cup soaked almonds. Strain liquid through a fine-mesh sieve or cheesecloth. Refrigerate covered for up to 3 days.

Stuffed Capsicums

Capsicums are just one of those vegetables that take on a different flavour once cooked. Tender and flavourful, these capsicums are stuffed with a blend of rice, tomatoes and seasonings with the addition of mushrooms, lending a "meaty" touch to this recipe.

- **Hands-On Time:** 15 minutes
- **Cook Time:** 20 minutes

Serves 3

2 medium capsicums, colour of choice
2 teaspoons olive oil
1/2 cup cooked brown rice
1/2 cup canned fire-roasted diced tomatoes, including juice
1/2 cup tomato sauce
3/4 tablespoon finely diced onion
1/4 cup chopped baby bella (cremini) mushrooms
2 teaspoons Italian seasoning
1/4 teaspoon smoked paprika
1/2 teaspoon salt
1/4 teaspoon freshly ground black pepper

1. Cut bell capsicums in half from top to bottom and seed them. For decorative flair, choose capsicums with a stem so that each half has a sliced stem. Brush inside and tops of capsicums with olive oil. Set aside.
2. In a medium bowl, combine rice, tomatoes, tomato sauce, onion, mushrooms, Italian seasoning, smoked paprika, salt and pepper.
3. Preheat air fryer at 180°C for 3 minutes.
4. Evenly distribute rice mixture among the capsicum halves.
5. Place two halves in the air fryer basket. Cook for 10 minutes.
6. Transfer to a serving plate. Continue with remaining halves. Serve warm.

PER SERVING

KILOJOULES: 359 | **FAT:** 2.5g | **PROTEIN:** 2.0g | **SODIUM:** 499mg | **FIBRE:** 2.8g | **CARBOHYDRATES:** 12.9g | **SUGAR:** 4.6g

One-Pot Wonders

Tuna Noodle Casserole

Tuna noodle casserole has been made for generations. The soft egg noodles are great with tuna, peas, celery and other fillings.

- **Hands-On Time:** 15 minutes
- **Cook Time:** 15 minutes

Serves 4

- 230 grams egg noodles, cooked
- 1/2 cup canned sweet peas, drained
- 300 grams can condensed cream of mushroom soup
- 1/4 cup sour cream
- 1/4 cup grated Parmesan cheese
- 1 1/2 tablespoons full-cream milk
- 3/4 tablespoon soy sauce
- 140 grams can tuna packed in water, drained
- 1 1/2 tablespoons minced onion
- 1 stalk celery, diced
- 1/4 cup panko bread crumbs
- 1 1/2 tablespoons butter, melted

1. Preheat air fryer at 190°C for 3 minutes.
2. In a medium bowl, combine egg noodles, peas, mushroom soup, sour cream, Parmesan cheese, milk, soy sauce, tuna, onion and celery.
3. Lightly spray or brush oil on a round cake barrel (accessory). Add noodle mixture. Scatter bread crumbs across the top and drizzle evenly with butter. Cook for 15 minutes.
4. Remove barrel from air fryer and let rest for 10 minutes. Serve warm.

PER SERVING

KILOJOULES: 1849 | **FAT:** 16.1g | **PROTEIN:** 19.5g | **SODIUM:** 995mg | **FIBRE:** 3.6g | **CARBOHYDRATES:** 50.9g | **SUGAR:** 3.4g

Ham and Potatoes au Gratin

Rich and creamy, salty and cheesy — these ham and potatoes au gratin are layered to indulgent perfection. Make sure you get those potatoes paper-thin to ensure their tenderness. A mandoline is a great tool for this job.

- **Hands-On Time:** 15 minutes
- **Cook Time:** 20 minutes

Serves 4

- 1/4 cup thickened cream
- 1/4 cup full-cream milk
- 2 large eggs
- 3/4 tablespoon plain flour
- 1 teaspoon salt
- 1 teaspoon freshly ground black pepper
- 1 teaspoon smoked paprika
- 2 medium potatoes, scrubbed and sliced paper-thin
- 1 cup diced cooked ham
- 1/2 cup grated Gruyère cheese
- 3/4 tablespoon butter, melted
- 3/4 tablespoon grated Parmesan cheese
- 3/4 tablespoon panko bread crumbs
- 3/4 tablespoon fresh thyme leaves

1. In a medium bowl, whisk milk, cream, eggs, flour, salt, pepper and paprika. Add potatoes. Using your hands, ensure that all sides of potato slices are coated.
2. Preheat air fryer at 190°C for 3 minutes.
3. Lightly spray or brush oil on a round cake barrel (accessory). Evenly distribute half of the potato slices. Pour half of the egg mixture over potatoes. Layer half of the ham and then half of the Gruyère cheese. Repeat layering.
4. In a small bowl, combine butter, Parmesan cheese, bread crumbs and thyme. Distribute over casserole. Cover barrel with aluminium foil.
5. Place barrel in air fryer basket. Cook for 15 minutes. Remove foil and cook for an additional 5 minutes.
6. Remove barrel from air fryer and let rest for 10 minutes. Serve warm.

PER SERVING

KILOJOULES: 1615 | **FAT:** 16.4g | **PROTEIN:** 21.3g | **SODIUM:** 1,272mg | **FIBRE:** 3.8g | **CARBOHYDRATES:** 37.1g | **SUGAR:** 3.4g

Chicken Potpie

There is just something magical about a chicken potpie. Is it the creamy filling loaded with chicken and vegetables, or is it the fluffy and crunchy biscuit topping? Maybe all of these contribute to the goodness, mixed in with a little dose of nostalgia.

- **Hands-On Time:** 15 minutes
- **Cook Time:** 15 minutes

Serves 4

Chicken Filling

3/4 cup chicken broth
1/4 cup full-cream milk
1 1/2 tablespoons plain flour
2 cups diced cooked chicken
410 grams canned mixed vegetables
1 1/2 tablespoons finely diced brown onion
3/4 tablespoon fresh thyme leaves
1/2 teaspoon salt
1/4 teaspoon freshly ground black pepper

Biscuit Topping

1 cup plain flour
1 1/2 teaspoons baking powder
3/4 teaspoon salt
1/4 teaspoon freshly ground black pepper
3 tablespoons full-cream milk
3/4 tablespoon butter, melted

1. In a large bowl, whisk together broth, milk and flour. Toss in chicken, mixed vegetables, onion, thyme, salt and pepper.
2. Preheat air fryer at 190°C for 3 minutes.
3. Lightly spray or brush oil on a round cake barrel (accessory). Add chicken mixture. Place barrel in air fryer basket and cook for 5 minutes.
4. While chicken is cooking, mix biscuit topping ingredients in a small bowl. When chicken mixture is ready, drop sticky spoonfuls over it. Cook for an additional 10 minutes.
5. Remove barrel from air fryer and let rest for 10 minutes. Serve warm.

PER SERVING

KILOJOULES: 1518 | **FAT:** 8.6g | **PROTEIN:** 29.9g | **SODIUM:** 1,297mg | **FIBRE:** 5.1g | **CARBOHYDRATES:** 37.1g | **SUGAR:** 1.9g

Chilli Casserole

This mild beef and bean chilli casserole is simply spiced with cumin and chilli powder. If you like a little heat in your chilli, feel free to add your favourite hot sauce or cayenne powder.

- **Hands-On Time:** 15 minutes
- **Cook Time:** 11 minutes

Serves 4

230 grams beef mince
1/2 small brown onion, peeled and diced
1 celery stalk, diced
450 grams canned kidney beans in chilli sauce
1/2 cup canned fire-roasted diced tomatoes, including juice
1/2 teaspoon ground cumin
1/2 teaspoon chilli powder
1/4 teaspoon salt
1 cup corn chips, lightly crushed
1/2 cup Mexican-blend grated cheese

1. In a large frying pan over medium-high heat, cook beef, onion and celery for 4–5 minutes until beef is no longer pink. Drain fat. Add beans including sauce, tomatoes including juice, cumin, chilli powder and salt.
2. Preheat air fryer at 180°C for 3 minutes.
3. Spoon beef mixture into a round cake barrel (accessory). Evenly distribute corn chips and top with cheese. Cook for 6 minutes.
4. Remove barrel from air fryer and let rest for 10 minutes. Serve warm.

PER SERVING

KILOJOULES: 933 | **FAT:** 10.7g | **PROTEIN:** 22.7g | **SODIUM:** 750mg | **FIBRE:** 9.2g | **CARBOHYDRATES:** 31.9g | **SUGAR:** 3.4g

Pork and Cheesy Mac

The tasty ground pork is a welcome addition to this three-cheese macaroni and cheese. The bread crumb topping is crisped to perfection by the air fryer in this compact casserole.

- **Hands-On Time:** 15 minutes
- **Cook Time:** 20 minutes

Serves 4

230 grams uncooked elbow macaroni
230 grams pork mince
1 medium carrot, peeled and diced
1 celery stalk, diced
110 grams cream cheese, at room temperature
1/4 cup fetta cheese, crumbled
1/4 cup shredded Cheddar cheese
1/4 cup full-cream milk
1/4 cup plain bread crumbs
3/4 tablespoon butter, melted

1 Add elbow macaroni to a pot of boiling salted water and cook according to package directions.

2 In a large frying pan over medium-high heat, cook pork, carrot and celery for 4–5 minutes until pork is no longer pink. Set aside.

3 Drain pasta and put in a large bowl. Add cream cheese, fetta cheese, Cheddar cheese and milk. Stir until the warm pasta melts the cheeses. Add pork mixture and stir.

4 Preheat air fryer at 190°C for 3 minutes.

5 Mix bread crumbs and butter together in a small bowl.

6 Spoon pasta mixture into lightly greased round cake barrel (accessory). Top with buttered bread crumbs. Cook for 15 minutes.

7 Remove barrel from air fryer and let rest for 10 minutes. Serve warm.

PER SERVING

KILOJOULES: 2133 | **FAT:** 18.7g | **PROTEIN:** 26.6g | **SODIUM:** 526mg | **FIBRE:** 3.4g | **CARBOHYDRATES:** 51.8g | **SUGAR:** 4.1g

Shepherd's Pie

The term shepherd's pie is incorrectly used on many menus. It should only be called this if it contains ground lamb, because a shepherd tended sheep. Mixed with vegetables and fresh herbs and topped with homemade mashed potatoes, this "pie" is hearty, healthy and comforting.

- **Hands-On Time:** 15 minutes
- **Cook Time:** 22 minutes

Serves 4

Potato Topping

1 large potato, peeled and diced
1 ½ tablespoons butter
1 ½ tablespoons full-cream milk
½ teaspoon salt
½ teaspoon freshly ground black pepper

Meat Filling

230 grams lamb mince
1 medium carrot, peeled and diced
¼ cup peas
¼ cup corn kernels
½ small brown onion, peeled and diced
1 tablespoon plain flour
⅔ cup tomato based sauce
1 teaspoon chopped fresh rosemary
1 teaspoon fresh thyme leaves
½ teaspoon salt
½ teaspoon freshly ground black pepper

1. Add diced potatoes to a medium pot of boiling salted water and cook for 4–5 minutes until fork-tender.
2. While potatoes are cooking, add lamb, carrot, peas, corn and onion to a large frying pan. Cook over medium-high heat for 4–5 minutes until lamb is no longer pink. Add flour, tomato sauce, rosemary, thyme, salt and pepper and combine.
3. Drain potatoes and transfer to a medium bowl. Add butter, milk, salt and pepper. Mash until smooth.
4. Preheat air fryer at 180°C for 3 minutes.
5. Spoon meat filling into lightly greased round cake barrel (accessory). Top with mashed potatoes. Using the tines of a fork, run shallow lines in the top of the potatoes for a decorative touch. Cook for 12 minutes.
6. Remove barrel from air fryer and let rest for 10 minutes. Serve warm.

PER SERVING

KILOJOULES: 1179 | **FAT:** 13.5g | **PROTEIN:** 13.9g | **SODIUM:** 1,005mg | **FIBRE:** 3.6g | **CARBOHYDRATES:** 24.7g | **SUGAR:** 4.7g

Green Chilli Chicken Casserole

This hearty casserole takes no time to put together. Serve with a salad to add more vegetables to the meal.

- **Hands-On Time:** 10 minutes
- **Cook Time:** 35 minutes

Serves 4

1 cup corn kernels
300 grams canned condensed cream of potato soup
200 gram can diced green chilli peppers
450 grams chicken breast tenders (or chicken breasts cut into strips)
¼ cup panko bread crumbs
¾ tablespoon butter, melted
¼ cup shredded Gouda cheese

WHAT ARE CHICKEN TENDERS?

Chicken tenders aren't just those deep-fried pieces of yuck found in kids' meals. They're actually part of the chicken breast. Each chicken has two of them. They are on the side of each breast, sometimes referred to as a "hanging tender". They are sold as chicken tenders; however, if you can't find any, don't worry. There is no taste difference between them and the breast, so just slice your own "tenders" if necessary.

1. In a small bowl, combine corn, potato soup and chilli peppers.
2. Preheat air fryer at 180°C for 3 minutes.
3. Add chicken tenders to lightly greased square cake barrel (accessory). Spoon corn mixture evenly over tenders. Cook for 25 minutes.
4. While chicken is cooking, combine bread crumbs and butter. When chicken is ready, sprinkle crumbs over chicken mixture and cook for an additional 5 minutes. Sprinkle cheese over casserole. Cook for an additional 5 minutes. Using a meat thermometer, ensure that chicken has an internal temperature of at least 75°C.
5. Remove barrel and let rest for 5 minutes. Serve warm.

PER SERVING

KILOJOULES: 1008 | **FAT:** 6.7g | **PROTEIN:** 19.8g | **SODIUM:** 750mg | **FIBRE:** 3.3g | **CARBOHYDRATES:** 25.0g | **SUGAR:** 5.3g

Mama's Little Lasagna

When you don't want a giant tray of lasagna to eat from for a week, make this little lasagna in your air fryer. Use oven-ready lasagna sheets and break them to fit each small layer.

- **Hands-On Time:** 15 minutes
- **Cook Time:** 24 minutes

Serves 4

230 grams Italian sausage, loose or removed from casings
¼ cup diced yellow onion
1 cup Napoletana Sauce (see page 66)
1 cup ricotta cheese
⅓ cup grated Parmesan cheese
1 large egg
2 teaspoons Italian seasoning
½ teaspoon salt
5 oven-ready lasagna sheets
1 cup grated mozzarella cheese

1. In a medium frying pan over medium heat, cook sausage and onion for 5–6 minutes until sausage is no longer pink. Drain fat. Stir in napoletana sauce. Simmer for 3 minutes.
2. In a small bowl, combine ricotta cheese, Parmesan cheese, egg, Italian seasoning and salt.
3. Lightly spray or brush oil on the square cake barrel (accessory).
4. Spoon a quarter of the meat mixture into barrel. Snap lasagna sheets to fit pan until you have a layer. Layer on a third of the ricotta mixture. Sprinkle a quarter of the mozzarella. Repeat two more times. Finish with the remaining meat sauce and then the mozzarella.
5. Preheat air fryer at 190°C for 3 minutes.
6. Cover lasagna with aluminium foil. Cook for 12 minutes. Remove foil and cook uncovered for an additional 3 minutes.
7. Remove lasagna from air fryer and let rest for 10 minutes. Slice and serve warm.

WHAT ARE OVEN-READY LASAGNA SHEETS?

Found in the same aisle as the rest of the pasta, these noodles will have "oven-ready" or "no-boil" on the packaging. There is no need to boil these prior to layering your lasagna, saving your fingertips from dealing with those hot pasta sheets. The heated sauce softens the sheets while your dish cooks, yielding a beautiful lasagna. No one will ever know!

PER SERVING

KILOJOULES: 554 | **FAT:** 34.0g | **PROTEIN:** 29.3g | **SODIUM:** 1,325mg | **FIBRE:** 2.3g | **CARBOHYDRATES:** 25.2g | **SUGAR:** 3.9g

Cheesy Meatless Spaghetti Pie

For those who don't like a lot of fuss or muss, try this simple cheesy meatless spaghetti pie. If you want to jazz it up, feel free to add onions or peppers or mushrooms.

- **Hands-On Time:** 10 minutes
- **Cook Time:** 16 minutes

Serves 4

230 grams spaghetti, cooked
2 cups Napoletana Sauce (see page 66)
3/4 tablespoon dried basil
1/2 cup ricotta cheese
1/4 cup shredded Parmesan cheese
1/4 teaspoon salt
2 large eggs, whisked
1/2 cup shredded mozzarella cheese

1. Preheat air fryer at 190°C for 3 minutes.
2. In a medium bowl, combine cooked spaghetti, napoletana sauce, basil, ricotta cheese, Parmesan cheese and salt.
3. Add spaghetti mixture to lightly greased round cake barrel (accessory). Pour whisked eggs over spaghetti mixture.
4. Cook for 12 minutes. Add mozzarella cheese. Cook for an additional 4 minutes.
5. Remove spaghetti pie from air fryer and let rest for 10 minutes. Slice and serve warm.

PER SERVING

KILOJOULES: 1719 | **FAT:** 11.2g | **PROTEIN:** 21.2g | **SODIUM:** 855mg | **FIBRE:** 4.5g | **CARBOHYDRATES:** 54.4g | **SUGAR:** 7.0g

Quick Chicken Enchiladas

This recipe can use that leftover cooked chicken from last night's roast chicken. Sometimes that day-after chicken can become a little dry, but these enchiladas will breathe new life into those leftovers for a fresh new meal!

- **Hands-On Time:** 10 minutes
- **Cook Time:** 6 minutes

Serves 2

1 cup shredded or chopped cooked chicken
130 grams canned chopped green chillies
½ teaspoon salt
¼ teaspoon ground coriander
2 cups enchilada sauce, divided
1 cup refried beans
4 (15cm) flour tortillas
1 cup shredded Gouda cheese
1 spring onion, trimmed and sliced
1½ tablespoons sour cream

1. In a small bowl, combine chicken, chillies, salt, coriander and ¼ cup enchilada sauce.
2. Add ½ cup enchilada sauce to bottom of the square cake barrel (accessory).
3. Spread ¼ cup refried beans in a line down the middle of each tortilla. Add a quarter of the chicken mixture to each. Top with 1 tablespoon shredded cheese on each tortilla. Roll tortillas and place seam side down in cake barrel. Top with remaining sauce. Sprinkle with remaining cheese.
4. Preheat air fryer at 180°C for 3 minutes.
5. Place enchiladas in air fryer basket. Cook for 6 minutes.
6. Transfer to a dish and allow to cool for 10 minutes. Serve warm garnished with sliced spring onions and a dollop of sour cream.

PER SERVING

KILOJOULES: 3259 | **FAT:** 28.4g | **PROTEIN:** 52.0g | **SODIUM:** 4,123mg | **FIBRE:** 12.3g | **CARBOHYDRATES:** 72.1g | **SUGAR:** 21.5g

Tuscan Beans and Sausage

By using sausage that has already been smoked and beans that are canned, you can cut down on the cooking time, making this simple bowl a perfect after-work meal.

- **Hands-On Time:** 10 minutes
- **Cook Time:** 12 minutes

Serves 4

400 grams smoked sausage, cut into 3cm sections

410 grams canned diced tomatoes, drained

440 grams canned cannellini beans, rinsed and drained

1/4 cup chopped baby spinach

1/4 cup chopped fresh basil

1/4 cup finely diced yellow onion

1. Preheat air fryer at 190°C for 3 minutes.
2. In a medium bowl, combine all the ingredients.
3. Add sausage mixture to lightly greased round cake barrel (accessory). Cook for 12 minutes.
4. Remove barrel from air fryer and let rest for 10 minutes. Serve warm.

PER SERVING

KILOJOULES: 1995 | **FAT:** 26.0g | **PROTEIN:** 21.3g | **SODIUM:** 1,018mg | **FIBRE:** 7.4g | **CARBOHYDRATES:** 32.8g | **SUGAR:** 3.3g

Simple Ravioli Lasagna

This is the easiest lasagna you'll ever make. The cheese and pasta are already present in ravioli, so why not take advantage of that and just layer the ravioli with meat sauce?

- **Hands-On Time:** 10 minutes
- **Cook Time:** 20 minutes

Serves 4

230 grams Italian sausage, loose or removed from casings

½ small brown onion, peeled and diced

2 teaspoons Italian seasoning

1 ½ cups Spicy Napoletana Sauce (see page 70)

260 grams packaged refrigerated four-cheese ravioli

½ cup mozzarella cheese

OTHER VARIETIES OF RAVIOLI

For variety, layer different kinds of ravioli. Whether you enjoy mushrooms, butternut pumpkin or one of the many types of meat-filled ravioli, give them all a whirl to find your favourite.

1 In a medium frying pan over medium-high heat, cook sausage and onion for 5–6 minutes until pork is no longer pink. Drain fat. Stir in Italian seasoning and spicy napoletana sauce. Simmer for 3 minutes.

2 Lightly spray or brush oil on the square cake barrel (accessory).

3 Add a third of the meat sauce. Layer half of the ravioli. Add another third of meat sauce. Top with half mozzarella cheese. Add a layer of remaining ravioli and then remaining meat sauce. Top with remaining mozzarella.

4 Preheat air fryer at 190°C for 3 minutes.

5 Cover lasagna with aluminium foil. Cook for 8 minutes. Remove foil and cook uncovered for an additional 3 minutes.

6 Remove lasagna from air fryer and let rest for 10 minutes. Spoon and serve warm.

PER SERVING

KILOJOULES: 1983 | **FAT:** 27.2g | **PROTEIN:** 21.4.0g | **SODIUM:** 1,215mg | **FIBRE:** 3.7g | **CARBOHYDRATES:** 34.2g | **SUGAR:** 4.6g

Desserts

Glazed Cinnamon-Apple Doughnut Bites

These luscious little cinnamon-apple bites are complemented with a simple glaze. They're easy to make and nice for a quick, sweet breakfast or served warm with a dish of creamy cinnamon ice cream after a nice meal.

- **Hands-On Time:** 10 minutes
- **Cook Time:** 11 minutes

Serves 5

Doughnut Holes

- 2/3 cup plain flour
- 1/8 teaspoon salt
- 1/2 teaspoon baking powder
- 1 teaspoon ground cinnamon
- 1 1/2 tablespoons light brown sugar
- 1/2 cup peeled, cored and grated Granny Smith apple (approximately 1 medium apple)
- 2 1/4 tablespoons full-cream milk
- 3/4 tablespoon butter, melted

Glaze

- 1 1/2 tablespoons icing sugar
- 1–2 teaspoons full-cream milk

1. In a medium bowl, combine flour, salt, baking powder, cinnamon and sugar.
2. Using paper towels, squeeze the moisture out of the shredded apple. Add to flour mixture. Add milk and butter. Stir until combined.
3. Preheat air fryer at 160°C for 5 minutes.
4. Form mixture into 10 (3cm) balls and add to lightly greased pizza pan (accessory). It's alright if they are touching. Cook for 11 minutes.
5. Transfer doughnut bites to a cooling rack.
6. When cooled, whisk together glaze ingredients in small bowl, 1 teaspoon milk at a time, until desired consistency, and then gently drizzle over doughnut bites.

PER SERVING

KILOJOULES: 560 | **FAT:** 2.6g | **PROTEIN:** 2.2g | **SODIUM:** 112mg | **FIBRE:** 1.1g | **CARBOHYDRATES:** 25.8g | **SUGAR:** 11.7g

Strawberry Shortcake

A few ordinary ingredients come together to create extraordinary buttery, flaky dough — the perfect foundation for your berry mixture. Spoon it on and top with fresh whipped cream.

- **Hands-On Time:** 15 minutes
- **Cook Time:** 20 minutes

Serves 4

450 grams fresh strawberries, stemmed and sliced
¼ cup sugar
1 teaspoon fresh lemon zest
1 cup thickened cream
1 ½ tablespoons icing sugar
2 cups plain flour
2 teaspoons baking powder
1 teaspoon salt
1 ½ tablespoons butter, melted
1 cup buttermilk

USE A STAINLESS-STEEL BOWL WHEN MAKING WHIPPED CREAM

A stainless-steel bowl, preferably chilled, will yield the beautiful peaks and fluffiness when making fresh whipped cream. The whipping process actually generates heat, and the chilled metal bowl helps the cream stay cold longer while whipping.

1. In a small bowl, combine strawberries, sugar and lemon zest. Refrigerate covered until ready to use.
2. In a metal bowl, beat together thickened cream and icing sugar for 1–2 minutes until medium peaks form. Refrigerate covered until ready to use.
3. In a medium bowl, combine flour, baking powder and salt. Add butter and buttermilk until a sticky dough forms.
4. Preheat air fryer at 180°C for 3 minutes.
5. Flour your hands and form mixture into four balls. Add to lightly greased pizza pan (accessory) and gently pat down to flatten the tops. The biscuits will be touching. Cook for 20 minutes.
6. Transfer biscuits to plates and cut each one in half. Add strawberry mixture and whipped cream to each biscuit bottom. Place the top part of the biscuit on whipped cream and serve.

PER SERVING

KILOJOULES: 2568 | **FAT:** 28.0g | **PROTEIN:** 10.9g | **SODIUM:** 914mg | **FIBRE:** 3.8g | **CARBOHYDRATES:** 77.6g | **SUGAR:** 26.4g

Confetti Cake

When you are celebrating something with two to four people, sometimes there is no need for an oversized sheet cake. This mini colourful cake is perfect for birthdays, anniversaries or just for happiness.

- **Hands-On Time:** 15 minutes
- **Cook Time:** 25 minutes

Serves 6

Cake

3 tablespoons butter, melted and cooled

3 tablespoons full-cream milk

1 teaspoon vanilla extract

2 large eggs

1¹⁄₄ cups plain flour

2 teaspoons baking powder

¹⁄₂ teaspoon baking soda

Pinch salt

¹⁄₃ cup rainbow sprinkles, plus extra for decoration

Buttercream Icing

1 cup icing sugar

¹⁄₄ cup butter, melted and cooled

¹⁄₂ teaspoon vanilla extract

³⁄₄ tablespoon full-cream milk

CREATE A FOIL SLING

You may want to make an aluminium-foil sling for easy pan retrieval. Take a 25cm × 25cm square of aluminium foil and fold it back and forth until you have a 5cm × 25cm sling. Place sling under the pan before cooking so that you can easily lift up the heated dish when cooking is complete.

1. In a small bowl, combine butter, milk, vanilla and eggs.
2. In a large bowl, combine flour, baking powder, baking soda, salt and ¹⁄₃ cup sprinkles.
3. Pour wet ingredients from the small bowl into the large bowl with dry ingredients. Gently combine ingredients. Do not overmix. Spoon mixture into greased round cake barrel (accessory). Cover with aluminium foil.
4. Preheat air fryer at 180°C for 3 minutes.
5. Cook for 15 minutes. Remove foil. Cook for an additional 10 minutes.
6. Remove cake pan from the air fryer and transfer to a rack until cool. Flip cake onto a serving platter.
7. Once cake has cooled, prepare buttercream icing by creaming together its ingredients in a small bowl. Spread icing over cake and garnish with extra rainbow sprinkles.

PER SERVING

KILOJOULES: 1548 | **FAT:** 18.5g | **PROTEIN:** 5.3g | **SODIUM:** 323mg | **FIBRE:** 0.7g | **CARBOHYDRATES:** 48.5g | **SUGAR:** 27.9g

Dark Chocolate Custard

It is so amazing how simple ingredients like eggs, sugar and milk can create such pure delight. Drop a dollop of fresh whipped cream on top of this custard with some chocolate curls for a fancy dessert fit for guests!

- **Hands-On Time:** 15 minutes
- **Cook Time:** 24 minutes

Serves 4

4 large egg yolks
1 ½ tablespoons sugar
Pinch salt
¼ teaspoon vanilla extract
¾ cup thickened cream
¾ cup full-cream milk
¾ cup dark chocolate chips

THE EASIEST DECORATIVE CHOCOLATE CURLS

There are many more complicated ways to make chocolate curls, but this method does the trick every time. You need two things — a bar of chocolate and a vegetable peeler. Hold chocolate on its side. Using medium pressure and going slowly, peel the side of the chocolate bar into curls. If your chocolate begins to soften, freeze it for a minute or two and continue.

1. In a small bowl, whisk together egg yolks, sugar, salt and vanilla. Set aside.
2. In a medium saucepan over medium-low heat, combine milk and cream and heat to a low simmer. Whisk a tablespoon of the warmed milk mixture into the egg mixture to temper the eggs, then slowly whisk egg mixture back into the saucepan with remaining milk and cream. Add chocolate chips and continually stir for 10 minutes on simmer until chocolate is melted. Remove from heat and evenly distribute chocolate mixture among four custard-sized ramekins.
3. Preheat air fryer at 180°C for 3 minutes.
4. Place two ramekins in air fryer. Cook for 7 minutes. Transfer ramekins to a cooling rack. Repeat with remaining two ramekins. Allow to cool for about 15 minutes. Then refrigerate covered for at least 2 hours before serving.

PER SERVING

KILOJOULES: 1527 | **FAT:** 22.7g | **PROTEIN:** 7.8g | **SODIUM:** 106mg | **FIBRE:** 1.1g | **CARBOHYDRATES:** 29.5g | **SUGAR:** 26.5g

Lemon Curd Palmiers

From the end result, these look impossible to make for a home chef, but they are actually quite simple, with layers of filo rolled up with "tart-tastic" lemon curd. Try orange curd for a change of pace.

- **Hands-On Time:** 15 minutes
- **Cook Time:** 24 minutes

Serves 6

3 teaspoons sugar, divided
1 sheet filo pastry, thawed to room temperature
¾ tablespoon butter, melted
⅓ cup lemon curd

HOMEMADE LEMON CURD

Although lemon curd can be purchased jarred in most grocery stores, it can be easily made and is amazingly delicious. Combine 4 large egg yolks and ½ cup sugar in a small pot over low heat. Whisk in ⅔ cup fresh lemon juice and 1 teaspoon fresh lemon zest. Slowly whisk in 4 tablespoons unsalted butter, 1 tablespoon at time. Stir continuously until combined and thickened. Strain through a sieve and store covered until ready to use for up to 1 week.

1. On a flat, clean surface sprinkle 2 teaspoons of sugar over surface. Place filo sheet over scattered sugar. Brush butter over sheet. Sprinkle with remaining sugar. Flip pastry.
2. Evenly spread lemon curd over sheet. Carefully roll one end toward the middle of sheet. Stop at the halfway point. Roll opposite side toward the middle. Refrigerate covered for 30 minutes.
3. Slice double log into 18 equal slices.
4. Preheat air fryer at 180°C for 3 minutes.
5. Place six palmiers in lightly greased air fryer basket. Cook for 8 minutes. Repeat with remaining palmiers.
6. Transfer cooked palmiers to a cooling rack. Serve warm or at room temperature.

PER SERVING

KILOJOULES: 502 | **FAT:** 4.6g | **PROTEIN:** 0.6g | **SODIUM:** 28mg | **FIBRE:** 0.1g | **CARBOHYDRATES:** 19.1g | **SUGAR:** 17.4g

Orange Cheesecake

The citrus in the orange is so fresh and bright, it helps make this a nice summer dessert. Change the flavour profile by using Choc Ripple biscuits or lemon cookies for the crust.

- **Hands-On Time:** 10 minutes
- **Cook Time:** 19 minutes

Serves 6

1 cup Arnott's Granita biscuits, crumbled
2 1/4 tablespoons butter, melted
340 grams cream cheese, at room temperature
1 1/2 tablespoons sour cream
2 large eggs
1/2 cup sugar
3/4 tablespoon fresh orange zest
3/4 tablespoon freshly squeezed orange juice
1 teaspoon vanilla extract
Pinch salt

1. In a small bowl, combine Granita crumbs and butter. Press into an 18cm springform pan.
2. In a medium bowl, combine cream cheese, sour cream, eggs, sugar, orange zest, orange juice, vanilla and salt until smooth. Spoon over biscuit base. Cover with aluminium foil.
3. Preheat air fryer at 200°C for 3 minutes.
4. Place springform pan into air fryer basket and cook for 4 minutes.
5. Reduce air fryer heat to 180°C, remove aluminium foil and cook for an additional 5 minutes.
6. The cheesecake will be a little jiggly in the centre. Refrigerate covered for a minimum of 2 hours to allow it to set. Release sides from pan and serve.

PER SERVING

KILOJOULES: 1690 | **FAT:** 25.5g | **PROTEIN:** 6.6g | **SODIUM:** 321mg | **FIBRE:** 0.6g | **CARBOHYDRATES:** 30.6g | **SUGAR:** 22.5g

Triple Chocolate Cheesecake

This dish has chocolate in the crust, the filling and the chocolate chip garnish. Most people might enjoy their slice with a tall glass of milk, but true chocoholics will pour themselves a glass of chocolate milk!

- **Hands-On Time:** 10 minutes
- **Cook Time:** 19 minutes

Serves 6

1 cup Arnott's Choc Ripple biscuit, crumbled
2 1/4 tablespoons butter, melted
340 grams cream cheese, at room temperature
1 1/2 tablespoons sour cream
2 large eggs
1/4 cup unsweetened cocoa powder
1/2 cup sugar
1 teaspoon vanilla extract
Pinch salt
1/4 cup mini chocolate chips

1. In a small bowl, combine choc ripple crumbs and butter. Press into an 18cm springform pan.
2. In a medium bowl, combine cream cheese, sour cream, eggs, cocoa, sugar, vanilla and salt until smooth. Spoon over chocolate biscuit crust. Cover with aluminium foil.
3. Preheat air fryer at 200°C for 3 minutes.
4. Place springform pan into air fryer basket and cook for 14 minutes.
5. Reduce air fryer heat to 180°C, remove aluminium foil and cook for an additional 5 minutes.
6. Remove cheesecake from air fryer. Garnish top with mini chocolate chips.
7. The cheesecake will be a little jiggly in the centre. Refrigerate covered for a minimum of 2 hours to allow it to set. Release from pan and serve.

PER SERVING

KILOJOULES: 1874 | **FAT:** 27.8g | **PROTEIN:** 7.8g | **SODIUM:** 327mg | **FIBRE:** 2.0g | **CARBOHYDRATES:** 36.4g | **SUGAR:** 25.9g

Mixed Berry and Apple Crumble

This streusel-like topping has oats, almonds and that rich brown sugar crisping up nicely in the air fryer. It's best served with vanilla ice cream or fresh whipped cream!

- **Hands-On Time:** 15 minutes
- **Cook Time:** 10 minutes

Serves 4

Filling

6 medium Granny Smith apples, peeled, cored and diced

1 cup thawed frozen mixed berries

3/4 tablespoon fresh lemon juice

1 1/2 tablespoons light brown sugar

1 teaspoon ground cinnamon

Pinch ground nutmeg

Pinch salt

Topping

3 tablespoons butter, melted

1 cup quick-cooking oats

1/8 cup plain flour

1/4 cup chopped almonds

1/4 cup packed light brown sugar

1/4 teaspoon sea salt

1 In a medium bowl, combine filling ingredients and place in lightly greased cake barrel (accessory).

2 In a small bowl, combine topping ingredients until crumbly. Spoon evenly over berry mixture.

3 Preheat air fryer at 180°C for 3 minutes.

4 Place cake barrel in air fryer basket. Cook for 10 minutes.

5 Transfer cake barrel to a cooling rack. Let cool for 10 minutes. Serve warm.

PER SERVING

KILOJOULES: 1924 | **FAT:** 16.4g | **PROTEIN:** 6.1g | **SODIUM:** 142mg | **FIBRE:** 8.1g | **CARBOHYDRATES:** 75.7g | **SUGAR:** 48.5g

MOVE OVER WONDER WOMAN

There are superfoods ... and then there are berries — super-superfoods! Rich in colour and taste, these little babies pack a punch with flavonoids, polyphenols, probiotics, antioxidants and vitamins.

Apple Pie Spring Rolls

These sweet cooked cinnamon apples are wrapped in crunchy goodness in every single bite. Enjoy these on the go or warmed and served with vanilla ice cream!

- **Hands-On Time:** 15 minutes
- **Cook Time:** 14 minutes

Serves 3

2 medium Granny Smith apples, peeled, cored and diced small

2 ¼ tablespoons butter, divided

½ teaspoon ground cinnamon

1 ½ tablespoons packed brown sugar

3 tablespoons pecan pieces

1 teaspoon lemon juice

Pinch salt

6 spring roll wrappers

1. In a large frying pan over medium heat, heat apples, 1½ tablespoons butter, cinnamon, sugar, pecans, lemon juice and salt. Cook for 4–5 minutes until apples are tender. Remove from heat and let rest for 5 minutes off the burner.
2. Drape a damp towel over stack of spring roll wrappers. Place one spring roll wrapper on a cutting board. Place approximately ¼ cup of apple mixture in a line in the middle of the wrapper. Fold 1cm of two sides of the spring roll toward the middle. Roll to form a spring roll and place seam side down in the air fryer basket. Repeat with remaining wrappers.
3. Preheat air fryer at 160°C for 3 minutes.
4. Place spring rolls in the air fryer basket. Cook for 3 minutes. Lightly brush tops of spring rolls with 1 tablespoon melted butter. Cook for an additional 6 minutes.
5. Transfer to a plate. Serve warm.

PER SERVING

KILOJOULES: 1836 | **FAT:** 17.7g | **PROTEIN:** 7.6g | **SODIUM:** 418mg | **FIBRE:** 4.0g | **CARBOHYDRATES:** 62.0g | **SUGAR:** 20.2g

Cinnamon Raisin Nutty Tarts

These sinful, sweet and warm pastries are filled with brown sugar, pecans, raisins and cinnamon and topped with vanilla ice cream.

- **Hands-On Time:** 10 minutes
- **Cook Time:** 27 minutes

Serves 6

1 1/2 tablespoons plain flour
3/4 cup chopped pecans
3/4 cup raisins
1 teaspoon ground cinnamon
1/4 cup packed brown sugar
1/2 tablespoons white sugar
Pinch salt
2 1/4 tablespoons butter
2 sheets puff pastry, thawed to room temperature
1 large egg, whisked
6 (1/2-cup) scoops vanilla ice cream

1. Use 1 tablespoon of flour to sprinkle on a flat, clean surface. Set aside the other tablespoon for your hands when you start working with the dough, as well as extra for the surface if needed.
2. In a small saucepan over medium-high heat, heat pecans, raisins, cinnamon, brown sugar, white sugar, salt and butter for 2–3 minutes until sugars are melted and mixture is creamy. Set aside to cool.
3. Preheat air fryer at 190°C for 3 minutes.
4. Place sheets of puff pastry on floured surface one at a time. Cut each sheet into six equal rectangles. Place approximately 1 1/2 tablespoons of mixture in the middle of each rectangle and spread it, leaving 1cm crust around perimeter uncovered. Create 12 tarts. Brush edges with whisked egg.
5. Add two tarts to lightly greased air fryer basket. Cook for 4 minutes. Transfer to a plate. Repeat until all tarts are cooked.
6. Serve warm with half a scoop of vanilla ice cream per two tarts.

PER SERVING

KILOJOULES: 1782 | **FAT:** 24.5g | **PROTEIN:** 5.5g | **SODIUM:** 106mg | **FIBRE:** 2.8g | **CARBOHYDRATES:** 46.7g | **SUGAR:** 31.5g

Lemon Cake

Don't underestimate the zest on a lemon. Yes, fresh lemon juice adds a beautiful citric quality, but the vibrant oils in the zest (or skin) of a lemon takes it a step further. Every bite of this small lemon cake bursts with big lemon flavour.

- **Hands-On Time:** 15 minutes
- **Cook Time:** 25 minutes

Serves 6

Cake

3 tablespoons butter, melted and cooled

3 tablespoons full-cream milk

½ teaspoon vanilla extract

2 large eggs

¾ tablespoon fresh lemon juice

¾ tablespoon fresh lemon zest

1 ¼ cups plain flour

2 teaspoons baking powder

½ teaspoon bi-carb soda

Pinch salt

Lemon Glaze

3 ¾ tablespoons icing sugar

4–5 teaspoons fresh lemon juices

ZESTING A LEMON

Use a microplane or the fine side of a box grater and rub the rind in one direction against the small blades. You will require a little precision to avoid the bitter white pithy layer. A sharp paring knife can be used as well and then finely chop the rind.

1. In a small bowl, combine butter, milk, vanilla, eggs, lemon juice and lemon zest.
2. In a large bowl, combine flour, baking powder, baking soda and salt.
3. Pour wet ingredients from the small bowl into the large bowl with dry ingredients. Gently combine ingredients. Do not overmix. Spoon mixture into greased round cake barrel (accessory). Cover with aluminium foil.
4. Preheat air fryer at 180°C for 3 minutes.
5. Cook for 15 minutes. Remove foil. Cook for an additional 10 minutes.
6. Remove cake pan from the air fryer and transfer to a rack until cool. Flip cake onto a serving platter.
7. Once cake has completely cooled, prepare glaze by whisking together its ingredients in a small bowl. Drizzle over cake. Slice and serve.

PER SERVING

KILOJOULES: 924 | **FAT:** 9.0g | **PROTEIN:** 5.2g | **SODIUM:** 216mg | **FIBRE:** 0.8g | **CARBOHYDRATES:** 28.2g | **SUGAR:** 7.4g

Nutella-Banana Pockets

Better than filled doughnuts, these buttery layered puff pastry pockets are treated with care in your air fryer, heating all sides into crunchy heaven.

- **Hands-On Time:** 10 minutes
- **Cook Time:** 20 minutes

Serves 6

1 1/2 tablespoons plain flour
2 sheets puff pastry, thawed to room temperature
1 cup Nutella
2 medium bananas, cut into 24 slices
1 large egg, whisked
3 teaspoons sugar

1. Use 1 tablespoon of flour to sprinkle on a flat, clean surface. Set aside the other tablespoon for your hands when you start working with the dough, as well as extra for the surface if needed.
2. Preheat air fryer at 190°C for 3 minutes.
3. Place a sheet of puff pastry on floured surface. Cut each sheet into six equal rectangles. Place 1 tablespoon of Nutella in the middle of each rectangle. Add 2 banana slices. Fold over so edges meet and lightly pinch the seams. Use a fork to pinch the borders to secure the seal. Create 12 puff pastry pockets. Brush the tops of each with whisked egg. Sprinkle each with 1/4 teaspoon sugar.
4. Add three pockets to lightly greased air fryer basket. Cook for 5 minutes. Transfer to a plate. Repeat until all are cooked. Serve warm.

PER SERVING

KILOJOULES: 1363 | **FAT:** 17.0g | **PROTEIN:** 4.7g | **SODIUM:** 66mg | **FIBRE:** 3.4g | **CARBOHYDRATES:** 46.7g | **SUGAR:** 31.9g

Cherry Filo Pastries

Sweet cherry season comes in like a wave and is gone too soon. But while it's here, enjoy the ride. These buttery little pastry pillows topped with supernutritional cherries are a treat that only comes around once a year.

- **Hands-On Time:** 20 minutes
- **Cook Time:** 19 minutes

Serves 4

2 cups quartered fresh sweet cherries, pitted
½ cup instant oats
¾ tablespoon packed light brown sugar
1 ½ tablespoons white sugar
½ teaspoon fresh lime zest
Pinch salt
Pinch ground nutmeg
8 filo sheets
1 ½ tablespoons butter, melted

1. In a medium saucepan over medium-high heat, cook cherries, oats, brown sugar, white sugar, lime zest, salt and nutmeg for 2–3 minutes. Remove from heat and let rest 5 minutes off the burner.
2. Lay out filo sheets on smooth surface. Place a damp towel over filo sheets so they won't dry out.
3. Retrieve one filo sheet from the pile. Lightly brush sheet with melted butter.
4. Place 2 tablespoons cherry mixture in the middle of the sheet, about 6cm from the bottom. Fold up the bottom of the sheet over the cherry mixture. Then fold the outside thirds lengthwise toward the middle, one at a time. Gently fold the pastry like a flag, forming a triangle each time. Brush the final end with butter to seal. Lightly brush completed triangle with butter. Set aside on a plate and continue with remaining pastries.
5. Preheat air fryer at 190°C for 3 minutes.
6. Place two pastries in air fryer basket. Cook for 4 minutes until lightly browned.
7. Transfer cooked pastries to a plate and continue with remaining ones. Serve warm or cooled.

PER SERVING

KILOJOULES: 1196 | **FAT:** 8.1g | **PROTEIN:** 5.0g | **SODIUM:** 221mg | **FIBRE:** 3.3g | **CARBOHYDRATES:** 48.8g | **SUGAR:** 19.7g

Island Filo Pastries

You can't get more island-style than fresh mango and sweet pineapple with a touch of lime. Of course, if you add a touch of the creamy and crunchy nature of the macadamia nut, then life is good.

- **Hands-On Time:** 20 minutes
- **Cook Time:** 23 minutes

Serves 5

3/4 cup diced fresh pineapple
3/4 cup diced fresh mango
1/3 cup honey
3/4 tablespoon sugar
2 teaspoons cornflour
1/4 teaspoon lime juice
1/4 cup crushed salted macadamia nuts
10 filo sheets
1/3 cup butter, melted

1. In a medium saucepan over medium-high heat, add pineapple, mango, honey, sugar, cornflour, lime juice and crushed nuts. Bring to a boil and then reduce to a simmer for 3 minutes. Remove from heat and let mixture rest for 5 minutes off the burner.
2. Lay out filo sheets on smooth surface. Place a damp towel over filo sheets so they won't dry out.
3. Retrieve one filo sheet from the pile. Lightly brush sheet with melted butter.
4. Place 2 tablespoons fruit mixture in the middle of the sheet, about 6cm from the bottom. Fold up the bottom of the sheet over the fruit mixture. Then fold the outside thirds lengthwise toward the middle, one at a time. Gently fold the pastry like a flag, forming a triangle each time. Brush the final end with butter to seal. Lightly brush completed triangle with butter. Set aside on a plate and continue with remaining pastries.
5. Preheat air fryer at 190°C for 3 minutes.
6. Place two pastries in air fryer basket. Cook for 4 minutes until lightly browned.
7. Transfer cooked pastries to a plate and repeat with remaining ones. Serve warm or cooled.

PER SERVING

KILOJOULES: 1581 | **FAT:** 18.4g | **PROTEIN:** 3.8 | **SODIUM:** 209mg | **FIBRE:** 2.1g | **CARBOHYDRATES:** 49.9g | **SUGAR:** 27.2g

Peanut Butter and Chocolate Brownies

If your sweet tooth is acting up but you don't want a huge tray of brownies, this small dish of treats will curb that craving without all the leftovers.

- **Hands-On Time:** 10 minutes
- **Cook Time:** 12 minutes

Makes 9 brownies

½ cup plain flour
1 ½ tablespoons unsweetened cocoa powder
⅓ cup sugar
¼ teaspoon bi-carb soda
2 ¼ tablespoons unsalted butter, melted
1 large egg
Pinch salt
¼ cup dark chocolate chips
⅓ cup peanut butter chips

1. In a medium bowl, combine flour, cocoa, sugar, baking soda and butter. Stir in egg and salt. Add chocolate chips and peanut butter chips. Mixture will be thick and sticky.
2. Preheat air fryer at 180°C for 3 minutes.
3. Press mixture into a greased square cake barrel (accessory).
4. Place pan into basket and insert into air fryer. Cook for 12 minutes. Remove pan from air fryer and let brownies cool for 10 minutes.
5. Slice into nine sections and serve warm or at room temperature.

PER SERVING

KILOJOULES: 707 | **FAT:** 8.4g | **PROTEIN:** 3.7 | **SODIUM:** 78mg | **FIBRE:** 1.2g | **CARBOHYDRATES:** 21.4g | **SUGAR:** 13.8g

Index

Note: Page numbers in **bold** indicate recipe category lists.

C

D

E

F

G

H

I

J

L

M

N

O

P

T